THE BUMPER BOOK OF JOKES

OVER 2000 JOKES

Illustrated By Glen Singleton

hinkler

Published by Hinkler Books Pty Ltd
45–55 Fairchild Street
Heatherton Victoria 3202 Australia
www.hinkler.com.au

hinkler

© Hinkler Books Pty Ltd 2011

Cover and text design: Pandemonium Creative
Prepress: Splitting Image
Typesetting: MPS Limited

ISBN: 978 1 7418 4769 7

Printed and bound in China

Contents

ANIMAL CRACKERS

What do you call a camel with no humps?
A horse.

What do you call a fish with no eyes?
Fsh.

What do you call a shy sheep?
Baaaashful.

What do you call two pigs who write letters to each other?
Pen-pals.

What happened to the cat who swallowed a ball of wool?
She had mittens.

What do cats put in cold drinks?
Mice cubes.

What's a frog's favourite drink?
Croaka-cola.

How did the skunk phone his mother?
On a smellular phone.

Why are four-legged animals bad dancers?
Because they have two left feet.

What do you call a duck with fangs?
Count Quackula.

What's big, grey and wears glass slippers?
Cinderelephant.

Why do elephants live in the jungle?
Because they can't fit inside houses.

What happened when the dog went to the flea circus?
He stole the show!

Must be something I picked up at the circus!

Did you hear the one about the dog running ten miles to retrieve a stick?
It was too farfetched.

How do you know when an elephant has been using your phone?
You've been charged for trunk calls.

What has four legs and flies?
A dead cat.

How do you make a slow racehorse fast?
Put it on a diet.

What do you call a cow that eats grass?
A lawn mooer.

What did the mouse say to the elephant?
Squeak.

What's big, grey and sings jazz?
Elephantz Gerald.

What do you call a snake that works for the government?
A civil serpent.

Did you know it takes three sheep to make a cardigan?
Hmmm. I didn't even know they could knit.

Why don't turkeys get invited to dinner parties?
Because they use fowl language.

What do you call an elephant that never washes?
A smellyphant.

What do dogs and trees have in common?
Bark!

What is a slug?
A snail with a housing problem.

What's a crocodile's favourite game?
Snap.

What kind of vehicles do pigs drive?
Pig-up trucks.

What's black and white and red all over?
A sunburned zebra.

What would you do if a bull charged you?
Pay him cash.

Why are elephants grey?
So you can tell them apart from canaries.

What do you call the red stuff between an elephant's toes?
A slow hunter.

What do you get when you cross a mountain lion and a parrot?
I don't know, but when it talks, you had better listen!

What do frozen cows do?
They give ice-cream.

Did you hear about the duck decorator?
He papered over the quacks.

How do sheep get clean?
They have a baaaaath.

What do you give to a horse with a sore throat?
Cough stirrup.

What do you get if you run a sparrow over with a lawn mower?
Shredded tweet.

What time is it when you see a crocodile?
Time to run.

What has four legs and goes 'Boo'?
A cow with a cold.

Did you hear about the performer who specialised in bird impressions?
He ate worms.

What did the 100 kilo parrot say?
Polly want a cracker, NOW!

What do you say to a hitchhiking frog?
Hop in.

What did the hen say when she saw scrambled eggs?
What a crazy mixed-up kid.

What did the snail say when he hitched a ride on the turtle's back?
Weeeeeeeeeeeeeeeeeeeee!!!!

What time is it when an elephant sits on your fence?
Time to get a new fence.

What happened when the Big Bad Wolf fell into Grandma's washing machine?
He became a wash and werewolf.

What's a pig's favourite ballet?
Swine Lake.

What do you get when you cross a chicken and a caterpillar?
Drumsticks for everyone!

What did the canary say when she laid a square egg?
Ouch!

Why do elephants have trunks?
Because they can't fit everything into a handbag.

What did Mr and Mrs Chicken call their baby?
Egg.

What do you get if you cross a skunk with a bear?
Winnie the Poo.

Why do giraffes have long necks?
Because their feet stink.

What animal drops from the clouds?
A raindeer.

Did you hear about the cannibal lioness?
She swallowed her pride.

How do cows count?
They use a cowculator.

What's small, brown and squirts jam?
A hamster eating a donut.

Why do birds fly south?
It's too far to walk!

What has six legs, bites, buzzes and talks in code?
A morse-quito.

What's a tadpole after it is five days old?
Six days old.

What's the favourite class for snakes?
Hiss-tory.

Why do mother kangaroos hate rainy days?
Because their kids have to play inside.

When is it bad luck to see a black cat?
When you're a mouse.

What do you get if you cross a duck with a rooster?
A bird that wakes you up at the quack of dawn!

Why are dogs like hamburgers?
They're both sold by the pound.

Why did the cow jump over the moon?
Because the farmer had cold hands.

What does a lizard wear on special occasions?
A rep-tie.

Ten cats were on a boat, one jumped off, how many were left?
None, they were all copycats!

What's an octopus's favourite song?
I want to hold your hand, hand, hand, hand, I want to hold your hand, hand, hand, hand.

How do you know that carrots are good for your eyesight?
Have you ever seen a rabbit wearing glasses?

What kind of doctor treats ducks?
A quack.

How do pigs get clean?
They go to the hogwash.

What type of fish is always sleeping?
A kipper.

How did the frog die?
It Kermit-ted suicide.

Where do cows go for entertainment?
The moovies.

What do you do if you come across an unconscious rodent?
Give it mouse to mouse.

Where would you find a dog with no legs?
Exactly where you left it.

Why do gorillas have big nostrils?
Because they have big fingers.

What's black and white and makes a terrible noise?
A penguin playing the bagpipes.

What do you call a sleeping bull?
A bulldozer!

What did the porcupine say to the cactus?
Are you my mother?

Why can't a leopard hide?
Because he's always spotted!

What is grey with sixteen wheels?
An elephant on roller skates!

What's the difference between a barking dog and an umbrella?
You can shut the umbrella up.

How does a jellyfish race start?
Get set.

What do you do when you see two snails fighting?
Nothing, you just let them slug it out.

What game do cows play at parties?
Moosical chairs.

What's an army of worms called?
An apple corps.

Why should you never kiss chickens?
Because they've got fowl breath.

What's grey, has four legs and a trunk?
A mouse going on holiday.

What's the definition of illegal?
A sick bird.

woof...
woof...
woof..woof

What do you get when you cross an elephant with a sparrow?
Broken telephone poles everywhere.

What is brown, has a hump and lives at the North Pole?
A very lost camel!

Why can't an elephant ride a tricycle?
Because they don't have thumbs to ring the bell!

What do you do with a blue whale?
Try to cheer him up!

Hickory dickory dock,
Three mice ran up the clock,
The clock struck one,
But the other two got away with minor injuries.

Name six things smaller than an ant's mouth?
Six of its teeth!

What do you call a fly when it retires?
A flew.

What happened when the cow jumped over the barbed wire fence?
It was an udder catastrophe!

Why was the father centipede so upset?
All of the kids needed new shoes!

Sheep 1: *'Baa.'*
Sheep 2: *'I knew you were going to say that.'*

What do you get when you cross a corgi with a clock?
A watchdog.

What do you call cattle that always sit down?
Ground beef.

ON A HILL...SOMEWHERE IN AUSTRIA

What's a cow's favourite film?
The Sound of Moosic.

When is the best time to buy a canary?
When it's going cheap.

Where do monkeys cook their dinner?
Under the gorilla.

Which animal never stops talking?
The yak.

What do you get when you cross a rooster with a steer?
A cock and bull story.

What did Thomas Edison Elephant invent?
The electric peanut.

What's smaller than an ant's mouth?
An ant's dinner.

Why did they cross a homing pigeon with a parrot?
So if it got lost it could ask for directions.

What happened to the snake with a cold?
She adder viper nose.

What did scientists say when they found bones on the moon?
The cow didn't make it!

What looks like half a cat?
The other half!

Why did the snail paint an S on its car?
So people would say, 'Look at that S car go!'

Where do you put a noisy dog?
In a barking lot!

What's the difference between an African elephant and an Indian elephant?
About 6,000 kilometres.

Where do baby elephants come from?
Very big storks.

Where do pigs go for their holidays?
Hamsterdam.

What shouldn't you do when you meet a shark?
Go to pieces.

Why did the cat put the letter 'M' into the freezer?
Because it turns 'ice' into 'mice'.

What can go as fast as a race horse?
The jockey!

How do goldfish go into business?
They start on a small scale.

What's big, white and furry, and found in outback Australia?
A very lost polar bear.

What's the difference between a well dressed man and a tired dog?
The man wears a suit, the dog just pants.

What did the skunk say when the wind changed direction?
Ahhh, it's all coming back to me now.

How do you stop an elephant from smelling?
Tie a knot in his trunk.

What's the biggest moth in the world?
A mam-moth.

How can you stop moles digging up your garden?
Hide the shovel.

Half an antelope....
RARE thanks

Why do tigers eat raw meat?
Because they can't cook.

Why don't cats shave?
Because they prefer Whiskas.

Why does a stork stand on one leg?
It would fall over if it lifted the other one.

Why did the goose cross the road?
To prove it wasn't chicken.

Why did Bo Peep lose her sheep?
She had a crook with her.

Who lives next to a horse?
His neigh-bours.

Where do sheep go on holiday?
Baaaali.

Which movie character do insects like best?
Bug Lightyear.

If horses wear shoes what do camels wear?
Desert boots.

Why do horses only wear shoes?
Because they would look silly with socks on.

How can you tell a rabbit from a gorilla?
A rabbit looks nothing like a gorilla.

Why do cows use the doorbell?
Because their horns don't work!

How do tell which end of a worm is the head?
Tickle him in the middle and watch where he smiles.

What do you call a monkey with a banana in each ear?
Anything, he can't hear you.

YOU *?@!+ MONKEY

How do bees travel?
They take the buzz!

Where do sheep go to get haircuts?
To the Baa Baa shop!

What would you get if you crossed a chicken with a mild-mannered reporter?
Cluck Kent.

What's black and white and hides in caves?
A zebra who owes money.

Why did the traffic officer book the sheep?
Because it did a ewe turn.

What's white on the outside, green on the inside, and hops?
A frog sandwich.

What's worse than finding a worm in your apple?
Finding half a worm!

What do you give a sick elephant?
A very big paper bag.

Why did the chicken join the band?
Because it had drumsticks.

Why did the koala fall out of the tree?
Because it was dead.

What do cats eat as a special treat?
Mice-creams.

Why can't frogs get life insurance?
Because they are always croaking.

What did one flea say to the other?
Shall we walk or take the dog?

How many skunks does it take to stink out a room?
A phew.

What should you know if you want to be a lion tamer?
More than the lion.

What did Tarzan say when he saw the elephants coming over the hill?
Here come the elephants over the hill.

Why did the lion spit out the clown?
Because he tasted funny.

What kind of dog tells time?
A watchdog!

Who is the king of the monkeys?
Henry the Ape.

What goes tick tick woof?
A watchdog.

What did the dog say when he sat on the sandpaper?
Rough, rough!

What did the giraffe say when a car load of tourists drove past?
It's terrible the way they're caged up.

Why did the shark take so long to eat a victim's arm?
Because the victim's watch made it time consuming.

Why does a tiger have stripes?
So it won't be spotted.

What do you call a penguin in the desert?
Lost.

How do you spell 'mouse trap' with three letters?
C A T.

DINOSAURS

How would you feel if you saw a dinosaur in your backyard?
Very old.

When did the last dinosaur die?
After the second-last dinosaur.

What's the hardest part of making dinosaur stew?
Finding a pot big enough to hold the dinosaur.

What do you get if you cross a dinosaur with a werewolf?
Who knows, but I wouldn't want to be within a thousand kilometres of it when the moon is full!

Is there a full moon tonight or tomorrow night?

How do dinosaurs pay their bills?
With Tyrannosaurus cheques.

What do dinosaurs put on their floors?
Rep-tiles.

What's worse than a Tyrannosaurus with a toothache?
A Diplodocus with a sore throat!

What do you call a dinosaur that destroys everything in its path?
Tyrannosaurus Wrecks.

What do you get if you cross a dinosaur with a termite?
A huge bug that eats big buildings for breakfast!

What do you get when you cross a Stegosaurus with a pig?
A porky spine.

What dinosaur is home on the range?
Tyrannosaurus Tex.

Why did the dinosaur not cross the road?
It was extinct.

Why couldn't the long-necked dinosaur see?
Because it had its head in the clouds!

What do you get when a dinosaur skydives?
A large hole.

What do you call a dinosaur with high heels?
My-feet-are-saurus.

What do you get if you cross a dinosaur with a vampire?
A blood shortage.

What do you get when you cross a dinosaur with a pig?
Jurassic Pork.

Which dinosaur was a famous author?
Charlotte Brontesaurus.

What do you call a scared tyrannosaurus?
A nervous rex.

What do you call a dinosaur eating a taco?
Tyrannosaurus Mex.

Why did the dinosaur fall out of a palm tree?
Because a hippopotamus pushed him out.

Why didn't the dinosaur cross the road?
Because roads weren't invented.

What do you get if you cross a dinosaur with a dog?
A very nervous mailman.

What do you call a dinosaur that's a noisy sleeper?
Brontosnorus.

What do you cut a dinosaur bone with?
A dino-saw.

Why did the baby dinosaur get arrested?
He took the bus home!

What's fifty-metres long and jumps every ten seconds?
A dinosaur with the hiccups.

Why do dinosaurs have flat feet?
Because they don't wear sneakers.

What's the scariest dinosaur of all?
The Terrordactyl.

What do you get if you give a dinosaur a pogo stick?
Big holes in your driveway.

Why are old dinosaur bones kept in a museum?
Because they can't find any new ones.

Which dinosaur does well in English exams?
Tyrannathesaurus Rex.

What do you call a dinosaur with magic powers?
Tyrannosaurus Hex.

What has a spiked tail, plates on its back and sixteen wheels?
A stegosaurus on roller skates.

What do you call a one-hundred-million-year-old dinosaur?
A fossil.

What does a Triceratops sit on?
Its Tricerabottom!

Where do dinosaurs go to the toilet?
In the dinosewer.

MONSTERS

Police Officer 1: *'Where's the skeleton?'*
Police Officer 2: *'I had to let him go.'*
Police Officer 1: *'But he's our main suspect.'*
Police Officer 2: *'I know. But I couldn't pin anything on him.'*

What do the guests do at a cannibal wedding?
Toast the bride and groom.

What do zombies use to make cakes?
Self-raising flour.

What does a cannibal say when a bus load of tourists drives past?
Smorgasbord.

What's Dr Jekyll's favourite game?
Hyde and seek.

How do you greet a three-headed monster?
Hello, hello, hello.

Did you hear about the monster who sent his picture to a lonely hearts club?
They sent it back, saying they weren't that lonely.

How did the monster cure his sore throat?
By gargoyling every day.

How do you know when there's a monster in your shower?
You can't close the shower curtain.

What kind of plate does a skeleton eat off?
Bone china.

Person 1: *'Why are you wearing garlic around your neck?'*
Person 2: *'It keeps away vampires.'*
Person 1: *'But there are no vampires.'*
Person 2: *'See, it works.'*

Which monster ate the three bears' porridge?
Ghouldilocks.

Why do skeletons drink milk?
Because it's good for the bones.

Where does Dracula keep his money?
In the blood bank.

Why are graveyards so noisy?
Because of all the coffin!

Little Monster: *'Should I eat my fries with my fingers?'*
Mummy Monster: *'No, you should eat them separately!'*

What happened when the abominable snowman ate a curry?
He melted.

What happened to Frankenstein's monster when he was caught speeding?
He was fined $50 and dismantled for six months.

What do you call a single vampire?
A bat-chelor.

What did the baby zombie want for his birthday?
A deady bear.

Why did they call the Cyclops a playboy?
Because he had an eye for the ladies!

Why do mummies have trouble keeping friends?
They're too wrapped up in themselves.

Who is big and hairy, wears a dress and climbs the Empire State Building?
Queen Kong.

What is Dracula's favourite fruit?
Necktarines!

Why did the monster buy an axe?
Because he wanted to get ahead in life.

Why was the monster catching centipedes?
He wanted scrambled legs for breakfast.

What do monsters make with cars?
Traffic jam.

What does a yeti eat for dinner?
An ice burger.

On which day do monsters eat people?
Chewsday.

Did you hear what happened to Ray when he met the man-eating monster?
He became an ex-Ray!

Did the bionic monster have a brother?
No, but he had lots of trans-sisters!

Did you hear about the cannibal who gnawed a bone for hours on end?
When he stood up, he fell over.

How does a yeti feel when it gets a cold?
Abominable.

What did the cannibal say to the explorer?
Nice to meat you.

What do vampire footballers have at half time?
Blood oranges.

What monster is the most untidy?
The Loch Mess Monster.

What do you call a four-metre monster?
Anything it likes.

What does a vampire never order at a restaurant?
Stake.

What's Dracula's car called?
A mobile blood unit.

What type of music do zombies like best?
Soul music.

What is red, sweet and bites people?
A jampire!

Why are skeletons usually so calm?
Nothing gets under their skin!

What do you call the winner of a monster beauty contest?
Ugly.

What bear goes around scaring other animals?
Winnie The Boo!

What is Dracula's favourite ice-cream flavour?
Vein-illa!

What kind of fur do you get from a werewolf?
As fur away as you can get!

What did the vampire say when he had bitten someone?
It's been nice gnawing you!

What do you get if you cross Frankenstein with a hot dog?
Frankenfurterstein.

What do you call a hairy beast in a river?
A weir-wolf.

What is a monster's favourite game?
Hide and Shriek.

How does Frankenstein eat?
He bolts his food down.

What type of horses do monsters ride?
Night mares.

Who is the best dancer at a monster party?
The Boogie Man.

What should you do if a monster runs through your front door?
Run out the back door.

Why did the cannibal live on his own?
He'd had his fill of other people.

What do vegetarian cannibals eat?
Swedes.

What do you think when you see a monster?
I hope he hasn't seen me!

Why don't cannibals eat weather forecasters?
Because they give them wind.

Why do vampires play poker?
Because they like playing for high stakes.

Who finished last at the Yeti Olympics?
Frosty the Slowman.

What's the favourite game at a cannibal's birthday party?
Swallow the leader.

What do you call a good-looking, kind and considerate monster?
A complete failure.

What do monsters have mid-morning?
A coffin break.

Why couldn't the skeleton go to the dance?
He had no body to go with.

What's a skeleton?
Someone with their outside off and their insides out.

Why did Godzilla get a ticket?
He ran through a stomp sign!

Why did the monster eat the North Pole?
He was in the mood for a frozen dinner!

What is the difference between a huge smelly monster and cake?
People like cake!

What time is it when a monster gets into your bed?
Time to get a new bed!

Why did the sea monster eat five ships carrying potatoes?
Because you can't just eat one potato ship.

What do you call a monster airline steward?
A fright attendant.

What do Italian monsters eat?
Spookgetti.

What eats its victims two by two?
Noah's Shark.

Why don't skeletons wear shorts?
Because they have bony knees.

25

What should you take if a monster invites you to dinner?
Someone who can't run as fast as you.

What's a good job for a young monster?
Chop assistant.

How can you help a hungry cannibal?
Give him a hand.

What did the cannibal say when he saw his wife chopping up a python and a pygmy?
Yum, snake and pygmy pie.

What do goblin children do after school?
Their gnomework.

What's a vampire's favourite dance?
The fangdango.

What song did the band play at the Demons and Ghouls ball?
'Demons are a Ghoul's Best Friend.'

What's three metres tall, has twelve fingers and three eyes, and wears sunglasses?
A monster on its summer holiday.

Who is King of the Cannibals?
Henry the Ate.

What do you call a twenty-tonne two-headed monster?
Sir.

How do you make a skeleton laugh?
Tickle his funny bone.

Where do skeletons keep their money?
In a joint account.

What do you do with a green monster?
Put him in a paper bag till he ripens.

What do you call a monster sleeping in a chandelier?
A light sleeper.

What is the best way to call Frankenstein's monster?
Long distance!

What happened to the monster that took the five o'clock train home?
He had to give it back.

If you crossed the Loch Ness monster with a shark, what would you get?
Loch Jaws.

What's the difference between a monster and a cookie?
Have you ever tried to dunk a monster in your milk?

Why are skeletons afraid of dogs?
Because dogs like bones.

Do zombies have trouble getting dates?
No, they can usually dig someone up.

What do Hungarian monsters eat?
Ghoulash.

What did the metal monster want on his gravestone?
Rust in Peace.

During which age did mummies live?
The Band-Age.

What is a monster's favourite drink?
Ghoul-Aid!

Who patrols cemeteries at night?
A fright watchman.

How do you greet a six-headed monster?
I didn't know you were twins.

What did the cannibal say when he saw Dr Livingstone?
Dr Livingstone, I consume.

What's a skeleton's favourite musical instrument?
A trom-bone.

Why do skeletons hate winter?
Because the wind just goes straight through them.

Why did the demon jump into the conserve?
Because he was a jammy devil.

Do zombies like the dark?
Of corpse they do.

Where do you find a skeleton's address?
In the bone book.

Why didn't the skeleton cross the road?
Because he didn't have the guts to!

What kind of boots do monsters wear?
Ghoulashes!

What is Dracula's favourite place in New York?
The Vampire State Building!

What do you get when you cross a vampire and a snowman?
Frostbite!

What do you get if you cross King Kong with a frog?
A huge gorilla that can catch a plane with its tongue!

CROAKKK

Why did it take the monster ten months to finish a book?
Because he wasn't very hungry.

What do sea monsters eat for lunch?
Potato ships!

Where do cannibals work?
At head office.

What do you do with a blue monster?
Try to cheer him up a bit.

How many monsters would it take to fill your living room?
How would I know? I'd leave as soon as the first one arrived!

Mr Cannibal: *'I've brought a friend home for dinner.'*

Mrs Cannibal: *'But I've already made a stew.'*

What does a boy monster do when a girl monster rolls her eyes at him?
He rolls them back to her.

What does a monster eat after he's been to the dentist?
The dentist.

What's a monster's favourite shape?
A vicious circle.

Does a monster need a menu while dining on a cruise ship?
No, just the passenger list.

What happened when the ice monster ate a spicy salsa?
He blew his cool.

What did Dracula call his daughter?
Bloody Mary.

Cannibal 1: *'How do you make an explorer stew?'*

Cannibal 2: *'Keep him waiting a few hours.'*

What type of music do mummies like best?
Ragtime.

What was the skeleton rock band called?
The Strolling Bones.

Why are Cyclops couples happy together?
Because they always see eye to eye.

Who won the running race between Count Dracula and Countess Dracula?
It was neck and neck.

Did you hear about the vampire comedian?
He specialised in biting satire.

Why isn't the Abominable Snowman scared of people?
Because he doesn't believe in them.

How many vampires does it take to change a light bulb?
None. They love the dark.

Why did the little monsters stay up all night?
They were studying for a blood test.

What do you call a dumb skeleton?
A numbskull.

What do you call a vampire's dog?
A blood hound!

What did the baby monster say to his babysitter?
I want my mummy!

How can you tell if a corpse is angry?
It flips its lid.

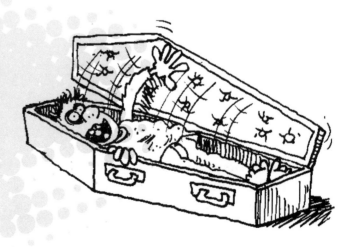

Who did the monster take to the Halloween dance?
His ghoul friend!

What do you think the tiniest vampire gets up to at night?
Your ankles.

Why did the monster comedian like playing to skeletons?
Because he knew how to tickle their funny bones.

How do you talk to the Loch Ness monster when he's so far under water?
Drop him a line.

Why didn't the skeleton and the monster fight?
The skeleton didn't have the guts.

What do you have to buy if you invite monsters around for a party?
A new house.

What is big, hairy, and bounces up and down?
A monster on a pogo stick!

What do monsters like reading in the papers every day?
Their horrorscopes, of course!

What does a monster mummy say to her kids at dinner time?
Don't speak with someone in your mouth.

Why did the monster eat his music teacher?
His Bach was worse than his bite.

Why did the vampire bite a computer?
Because he wanted to get on the interneck.

Was Dracula ever married?
No, he was a bat-chelor!

Why didn't the skeleton bother to defend itself in court?
Because it didn't have a leg to stand on.

What do little zombies play?
Corpses and robbers.

Why did the cannibal eat the missionary?
Because he'd developed a taste for Christianity.

What's a vampire's favourite sport?
Batminton.

What did Quasimodo become after he died?
A dead ringer.

What do you call a monster that was locked in the freezer overnight?
A cool ghoul!

How can you tell Martians would be good gardeners?
They all have green thumbs!

How does a monster count to thirteen?
On his fingers.

What don't zombies wear on boat trips?
Life jackets.

What did the alien say to the kettle?
Take your hand off your hip when I'm talking to you.

What do you get if you cross a vampire with Al Capone?
A fangster!

Why did the vampire go to the orthodontist?
To improve his bite.

What do you think of Dracula films?
Fangtastic!

Did you hear about the ghouls' favourite hotel?
It had running rot and mould!

Did you hear about the monster who lost all his hair in the war?
He lost it in a hair raid.

Why did the young monster knit herself three socks?
She grew another foot.

What's the name of a clever monster?
Frank Einstein.

What does a monster call his parents?
Dead and mummy.

How does a skeleton call his friends?
On a telebone.

a silly old sucker

What do you call an old and foolish vampire?
A silly old sucker!

What do baby sea monsters play with?
Sea-saws.

What did the monster say when he saw a rush-hour train full of passengers?
Great! A chew-chew train!

Why didn't the skeleton want to go to work?
Because his heart wasn't in it.

Why did the executioner go to work early?
To get a head start.

Why did the cannibal kidnap the tourist?
He wanted takeaway.

What does a devil do to keep fit?
Exorcise.

How does Dracula eat his food?
In bite-sized pieces.

What did the alien say to her son when he returned home?
Where on Earth have you been?

What did the witch say to the vampire?
Get a life.

What does a monster say when introduced?
Pleased to eat you.

What kind of cheese do monsters eat?
Monsterella!

Why is the vampire so unpopular?
Because he is a pain in the neck!

Why did the zombie decide to stay in his coffin?
He felt rotten.

Mum, everyone at school calls me a werewolf.
Ignore them and comb your face.

Little Monster: '*I hate my teacher's guts!*'
Mummy Monster: '*Then just eat around them!*'

Where do monsters send their clothes for cleaning?
The dry screamers.

Why can't the Invisible Boy pass school?
The teacher always marks him absent!

Did you hear about the vampire who got taken away in a straightjacket?
He went batty.

Let's rap!

What is a mummy's favourite kind of music?
Rap!

Why did the young vampire follow his dad's profession?
Because it was in his blood.

What did Frankenstein do when he saw the monster catcher approaching?
He bolted.

What did the cannibal say when he was full?
I couldn't eat another mortal.

Why doesn't anyone kiss vampires?
Because they have bat breath.

Mother vampire to son:
'Hurry up and eat your breakfast before it clots.'

Whats green, sits in the corner and cries?
The Incredible Sulk.

Where does Frankenstein's wife have her hair done?
At an ugly parlour.

How does an alien congratulate someone?
He gives him a high six.

What do you call a detective skeleton?
Sherlock Bones.

Why do dragons sleep during the day?
So they can fight knights!

Who brings the monsters their babies?
Frankenstork!

Why do skeletons play the piano in church?
Because they don't have any organs!

What do you call a monster that comes to collect your laundry?
An undie-taker.

What did the sea monster say when it saw the brand new ocean liner sail past?
Yum. Launch time.

What is Count Dracula's favourite snack?
A fangfurter!

Why did the troll tell jokes to the mirror?
He wanted to see it crack up!

How do you stop a charging monster?
Take away his credit card.

How do monsters like their eggs?
Terrifried.

Why did the monster eat the light bulb?
He wanted some light refreshment.

What do vampires gamble with?
Stake money!

What is a monster's favourite craft?
Tie and die.

Why did the monster paint himself in rainbow-coloured stripes?
He wanted to hide in a crayon box.

Why was the scary two-headed monster top of the school class?
Because two heads are better than one.

Why did the young monster take a runner to school in his lunch?
Because he liked fast food.

SCHOOL

Who was the fastest runner in the whole world?
Adam, because he was the first in the human race.

Name an animal that lives on the tundra.
A reindeer.
Name another.
Another reindeer.

Teacher: *'I hope I didn't see you copying from John's exam paper, James.'*
James: *'I hope you didn't see me either!'*

Teacher: *'Max, why are you late?'*
Max: *'The train had a flat tyre.'*

What do you call someone who greets you at the school door every morning?
Matt!

History teacher: *'What's the best thing about history?'*
Mary: *'All the dates.'*

Mum, I'm not going to school today.
Why not?
Because it's Sunday.

How many apples can you put in an empty box?
One. After that it's not empty anymore.

What word is always spelled incorrectly?
Incorrectly.

Teacher: *'Are you good at arithmetic?'*
Mary: *'Well, yes and no.'*
Teacher: *'What do you mean, yes and no?'*
Mary: *'Yes, I'm no good at arithmetic.'*

Why is the Mississippi such an unusual river?
It has four eyes and can't even see.

Gee...the Mississippi really does have four eyes!

First teacher: *'What's wrong with young Jimmy today? I saw him running around the playground, screaming and pulling at his hair.'*

Second teacher: *'Don't worry. He's just lost his marbles.'*

English teacher: *'James, give me a sentence with the word "counterfeit" in it.'*

James: *'I wasn't sure if she was a centipede or a millipede, so I had to count her feet.'*

History teacher: *'Why were ancient sailing ships so eco-friendly?'*

Student: *'Because they could go for hundreds of miles to the galleon.'*

Did you hear about the student who said he couldn't write an essay on goldfish because he didn't have any waterproof ink?

What birds are found in Portugal?
Portu-geese.

'I hope you're not one of those boys who sits and watches the school clock,' said the principal to the new boy.

'No, sir,' he replied. *'I have a digital watch that beeps at 3.15!'*

Our teacher talks to herself in class. Does yours?

Yes, but she doesn't realise it. She thinks we're listening!

Did you hear about the cross-eyed teacher?
He couldn't control his pupils.

History teacher: *'Here is a question to check that you did your homework on British kings and queens. Who came after Mary?'*

Student: *'Her little lamb.'*

In which class do you learn how to shop for bargains?
Buy-ology.

Science teacher: *'What are nitrates?'*
Student: *'Cheaper than day rates.'*

Dad, I's been expelled.
What? We spend a fortune on sending you to an exclusive private school and you still say 'I's'.

History teacher: *'What was Camelot?'*
Student: *'A place where camels are parked.'*

Teacher: *'Why can't you answer any of my questions in class?'*
Student: *'If I could, there wouldn't be much point in me being here.'*

Teacher: *'What's the name of a liquid that won't freeze?'*
Student: *'Hot water.'*

What is the easiest way to get a day off school?
Wait until Saturday.

Teacher: *'Why are you eating cake in my classroom?'*
Ed: *'Because the shop had run out of gum.'*

Maths teacher: *'Anne, why have you brought a picture of the queen of England with you today?'*
Anne: *'You told us to bring a ruler with us.'*

Teacher: *'Jessica, you aren't paying attention to me. Are you having trouble hearing?'*
Jessica: *'No, I'm having trouble listening.'*

Why did the student stand on his head?
To turn things over in his mind.

Teacher: *'I wish you'd pay a little attention.'*
Student: *'I'm paying as little attention as possible.'*

Geography teacher: *'What's the coldest country in the world?'*
Student: *'Chile.'*

Which word if pronounced right is wrong and if pronounced wrong is right?
Wrong.

Cookery teacher: *'Helen, what are the best things to put in a fruitcake?'*
Helen: *'Teeth.'*

Why did the teacher wear sunglasses?
Because his students were so bright.

Parent: *'In my day we didn't have computers at school to help us.'*
Child: *'You mean you got your schoolwork wrong all on your own?'*

What do you get if you cross a teacher and a traffic police officer?
Someone who gives you 500 double lines for being late.

What do you call an art teacher who is always complaining?
Mona Lisa.

Did you hear about the teacher who locked the school band in a deep freeze?
They wanted to play really cool jazz.

Mother: *'I told you not to eat cake before supper.'*
Son: *'But it's part of my homework, see: If you take an eighth of a cake from a whole cake, how much is left?'*

History teacher: *'Why do we refer to the period around 1000 years AD as the Dark Ages?'*
Student: *'Because there were so many knights.'*

Teacher: *'Sue, what letter comes after the letter "A"?'*
Sue: *'The rest of them.'*

What's the centre of gravity?
The letter 'V'.

Ben's teacher thinks Ben is a wonder child. She wonders whether he'll ever learn anything.

What is a runner's favourite subject in school?
Jog-raphy!

Why did the boy throw his watch out of the window during a test?
Because he wanted to make time fly.

When do clocks die?
When their time's up.

Maths teacher: *'Paul. If you had five pieces of chocolate and Sam asked for one of them, how many would you have left?'*
Paul: *'Five.'*

Have you heard about the gym teacher who ran around exam rooms, hoping to jog students' memories?

What fur do we get from a tiger?
As fur as possible.

Father: *'How do you like going to school?'*
Son: *'Going and coming home are fine; it's the part in the middle I don't like!'*

Teacher: *'Be sure to go straight home after school.'*
Student: *'I can't. I live around the corner!'*

Teacher: *'Can anyone tell me what the Dog Star is?'*
Student: *'Lassie.'*

How many letters are in the alphabet?
Eleven. Count them – t-h-e-a-l-p-h-a-b-e-t!

Woman 1: *'Your son is terribly spoiled.'*
Woman 2: *'How dare you. He's not spoiled at all.'*
Woman 1: *'Yes he is. He just got hit by a school bus.'*

Teacher: *'You missed school yesterday, didn't you?'*
Student: *'Not very much.'*

Teacher: *'I told you to draw a cow eating grass, but you've only drawn a cow.'*
Student: *'The cow has eaten all the grass.'*

Teacher: *'What came after the Stone Age and the Bronze Age?'*
Student: *'The saus-age.'*

Miss! I know what comes after the BRONZE AGE! The BAGG-AGE then the COTT-AGE followed by the GARB-AGE

Now students... I'm going to turn myself into...

sub-atomic particles

Did you hear about the technology teacher who left teaching to try to make something of himself?

Never go to school on an empty stomach. Go on the bus instead.

Did you hear about the teacher who wore sunglasses to give out exam results?
He took a dim view of his students' performance.

English teacher: *'Spell Mississippi.'*
Student: *'The river or the state?'*

What are the names of the small rivers that run into the Nile?
The juve-niles.

What is higher without the head than with it?
A pillow.

Have you heard about the sewing teacher who had her pupils in stitches?

Teacher: *'Did you know the bell had gone?'*
Sue: *'I didn't take it, Miss.'*

How does a maths teacher know how long she sleeps?
She takes a ruler to bed.

Student to teacher: *'I don't want to worry you but my dad said that if my grades don't improve, someone's going to get a spanking.'*

'What were you before you started school, girls and boys?' asked the teacher, hoping that someone would say, *'babies'*. She was disappointed when all the children cried out, *'Happy!'*

Playing truant from school is like having a credit card. Lots of fun now, pay later.

Where is the English Channel?
Not sure. It's not on my TV.

Principal: *'You should have been here at 9 am.'*
Student: *'Why, what happened?'*

Why was the principal worried?
Because there were so many rulers in the school.

How does a boat show its affection?
By hugging the shore.

What type of instruments did the early Britons play?
The Anglo-saxophone.

43

Simple Simon was writing a geography essay for his teacher. It began like this:

The people who live in Paris are called parasites . . .

Why can you believe everything a bearded teacher tells you?
They can't tell bald-faced lies.

Hey teacher, I'd hate to be grossly underpaid for my work. Does it bother you?

Teacher: *'If I bought 100 buns for a dollar, what would each bun be?'*
Student: *'Old and stale.'*

Teacher to parent: *'David's career choice as a train driver will suit him well. He has more experience of lines than any other student at this school!'*

Hey, did you see who stole my computer?
Yes, he went data way!

Maths teacher: *'If you multiplied 1386 by 395, what would you get?'*
Student: *'The wrong answer.'*

Hey teacher, I'd love to stick it out through the rest of class but I have a life.

'I'm not going to school today,' said Alexander to his mother. *'The teachers bully me and the boys don't like me.'*
'That's not too surprising. You're 35 years old,' replied his mother, *'and you're the principal!'*

Where do you find the biggest spider?
In the world wide web.

Teacher: *'Why haven't you been to school for the last two weeks, Billy?'*
Billy: *'It's not my fault – whenever I go to cross the road outside, there's a man with a sign saying, "Stop Children Crossing"!'*

Teacher: 'If you had one dollar and asked your dad for one dollar, how much money would you have?'

Student: 'One dollar.'

Teacher: 'Are you sure?'

Student: 'Yes, my dad wouldn't give me a dollar.'

What's the difference between a train station and a teacher?
One minds the train, the other trains the mind.

'What are three words most often used by students?' the teacher asked the class.

'I don't know,' sighed a student.

'That's correct!' said the teacher.

What is the robot teacher's favourite part of school?
Assembly.

Hey teacher, the class isn't really that dull … just you.

Teacher: 'What bird doesn't build its own nest?'

Student: 'The cuckoo.'

Teacher: 'That's right. How did you know that?'

Student: 'Everyone knows cuckoos live in clocks!'

Teacher: 'What family does the octopus belong to?'

Student: 'Nobody's I know.'

English teacher: 'Jamie, give me a sentence beginning with "I".'

Jamie: 'I is …'.

Teacher: 'No Jamie, you must always say "I am".'

Jamie: 'Okay. I am the ninth letter of the alphabet.'

Teacher: 'That's three times I've asked you a question. Why won't you reply?'

Student: 'Because you told me not to answer you back .'

Obviously the teacher didn't think my joke was too funny!

DETENTION CORNER

Laugh, and the class laughs with you. But you get detention alone.

Dad: *'How did you find your maths exam?'*
Son: *'Unfortunately, it wasn't lost!'*

Maths teacher: *'Richard, if you had 50 cents in each trouser pocket, and $2 in each jacket pocket, what would you have?'*
Richard: *'Someone else's clothes, sir.'*

Shane: *'Dad, today my teacher yelled at me for something I didn't do.'*
Dad: *'What did he yell at you for?'*
Shane: *'For not doing my homework.'*

Why are maths teachers good at solving detective stories?
They're quick at adding up clues.

Did you hear about the two history teachers who were dating?
They go to restaurants to talk about old times.

What do you call a teacher with a school on his head?
Ed.

Teacher: *'Billy, stop making ugly faces at the other students!'*
Billy: *'Why?'*
Teacher: *'Well, when I was your age, I was told that if I kept making ugly faces, my face would stay that way.'*
Billy: *'Well, I can see you didn't listen.'*

Science teacher: *'Which travels faster, heat or cold?'*
Student: *'Heat, because you can catch a cold.'*

Father: *'I want to take my girl out of this terrible maths class.'*
Teacher: *'But she's top of the class!'*
Father: *'That's why it must be a terrible class!'*

My teacher says I've got such bad handwriting that I ought to be a doctor!

Does that say... REMOVE APPENDIX .... or TAKE 1 TABLET 3 TIMES A DAY BEFORE MEALS?

DOCTOR'S SURGERY

MEDICAL REPORT

Did you hear about the maths teacher who wanted to order pizza for dinner, but was divided about whether to have additional cheese?

How many aerobics teachers does it take to change a light bulb?
Five, one to change it, the others to say, 'A little to the left, a little to the right, a little to the left, a little to the right.'

What is an English teacher's favourite fruit?
The Grapes of Wrath.

When Dad came home, he was amazed to see his son sitting on a horse, writing something.
'What are you doing up there?' he asked.
'Well, the teacher told us to write an essay on our favourite animal,' replied the boy.

Teacher: *'I told you to stand at the end of the line.'*
Student: *'I tried, but there was someone already there.'*

'Mary,' said her teacher. *'You can't bring that lamb into class. What about the smell?'*
'Oh, that's all right Miss,' replied Mary. *'It'll soon get used to it.'*

You're so dumb, when your teacher said she wanted you to get ahead, she really meant 'a head'.

Computer teacher: *'Sarah, give me an example of software.'*
Sarah: *'A floppy hat.'*

Student 1: *'We bought our retiring science teacher a gift – toilet water that cost $20.'*
Student 2: *'What! I would've sold you water from our toilets for only $2!'*

You'd make a good exchange student.
Do you think so?
Yes we might be able to exchange you for someone nice.

Teacher: *'That's the stupidest boy in the whole school.'*
Mother: *'That's my son.'*
Teacher: *'Oh! I'm so sorry.'*
Mother: *'You're sorry?'*

'What do you like about your new school, Billy?' asked Uncle Ned.
'When it's closed!'

'How old would you say I am, Francis?' the teacher asked.
'Forty,' said the boy promptly.
'What makes you think I'm 40?' asked the puzzled teacher.
'My big brother is 20,' he replied, *'and you're twice as silly as he is!'*

What did the buffalo say to his son when he went away on a long trip?
Bison.

Student: *'Where can I find out about ducks?'*
Librarian: *'Try the ducktionary.'*

What would you get if you crossed a teacher with a vampire?
Lots of blood tests.

Hey teacher, that last lesson you gave us was wonderful. Just one question: What were you talking about?

What do you know about the Dead Sea?
Dead? I didn't even know it was sick!

Student: *'I don't think I deserve a zero on this test.'*
Teacher: *'Neither do I, but it was the lowest I could give you!'*

Mother: *'Did you get a good place in the geography test?'*

Daughter: *'Yes, I sat next to the cleverest kid in the class.'*

Teacher: *'Why didn't you answer me, Stuart?'*

Stuart: *'I did, I shook my head.'*

Teacher: *'You don't expect me to hear it rattling from here, do you?'*

Teacher: *'Your daughter's only five and she can spell her name backwards! Why, that's remarkable!'*

Mother: *'Yes, we're very proud of her.'*

Teacher: *'And what is your daughter's name?'*

Mother: *'Anna.'*

Student: *'Would you punish someone for something they didn't do?'*

Teacher: *'Of course not.'*

Student: *'Good, because I didn't do my homework.'*

What kind of tests do witch teachers give?
Hex-aminations.

Dad, can you write in the dark?
I suppose so.
Good. Can you sign my report card, please?

Teacher: *'I'd like you to be very quiet today, girls. I've got a dreadful headache.'*

Mary: *'Please Miss, why don't you do what Mum does when she has a headache?'*

Teacher: *'What's that?'*

Mary: *'She sends us out to play!'*

What word is always spelled wrong?
Wrong.

Student: *'I didn't do my homework because I lost my memory.'*

Teacher: *'When did this start?'*

Student: *'When did what start?'*

ANIMAL ANTICS

What is white, lives in the Himalayas and lays eggs?
The Abominable Snow Chicken.

What did the rabbit give his girlfriend when they got engaged?
A 24-carrot ring.

What's the difference between a gym teacher and a duck?
One goes quick on its legs and the other goes quack on its legs!

How can you tell the difference between a rabbit and a monster?
Ever tried getting a monster into a rabbit hutch?

What did the lion say to his cubs when he taught them to hunt?
Don't walk across the road until you see the zebra crossing.

What do you call a lion wearing a hat?
A dandy lion.

What flies around your light at night and can bite off your head?
A tiger moth.

Where do elephants go on holidays?
Tuscany.

Do you know where to find elephants?
Elephants don't need finding – they're so big they don't get lost.

What's the healthiest insect?
A vitamin bee.

What lies down a hundred feet in the air?
A centipede.

What flies through the jungle singing operetta?
The parrots of Penzance.

How's a parrot supposed to sing operetta in a get-up like this?

What did the lion say when a car load of tourists drove past?
Meals on wheels.

What's the best advice a mother worm can give to her children?
Sleep late.

How do you get down from an elephant?
You don't get down from an elephant, you get down from a duck.

What did the goose say when she got cold?
I have people-bumps!

How can you tell an elephant from a banana?
Try to lift it up. If you can't, it's either an elephant or a very heavy banana.

What's the difference between a piano and a fish?
You can tune a piano, but you can't tuna fish!

Where do sheep buy shears?
At a baaaardware store.

Why did the bat miss the train?
Because it spent too long hanging around.

What disease do you have if you're allergic to horses?
Bronco-itis.

Why is an elephant large, grey and wrinkled?
Because if it was small, white and smooth it would be an aspirin!

What do you get when you cross an elephant with peanut butter?
Either an elephant that sticks to the roof of your mouth or peanut butter that never forgets.

What's bright blue and very heavy?
An elephant holding its breath.

What did one bee say to her nosy neighbour bee?
Mind your own bees' nest!

What do you get if you cross a parrot with a shark?
A bird that will talk your ear off!

What's slimy, tastes of raspberry, is wobbly and lives in the sea?
A red jellyfish.

What do you call a camel with three humps?
Humphrey.

Why do elephants never get rich?
Because they work for peanuts.

A grizzly bear walks into a bar and says to the bartender, *'I'll have a gin .... and tonic.'*

Bartender: *'What's with the big pause?'*

Bear: *'I don't know. My father had them, too.'*

What has an elephant's trunk, a tiger's stripes, a giraffe's neck and a baboon's bottom?
A zoo.

What do you get when you cross a shark with a crocodile and a Tyrannosauraus Rex?
I don't know, but don't take it swimming.

What do you get when you cross a seagull with a pair of wheels?
A bi-seagull.

What do you call a chicken that lays light bulbs?
A battery hen.

Why did the dinosaur cross the road?
Because there were no chickens.

Where does a dinosaur cross a busy 6 Lane motorway? Anywhere it likes!!

What happened when the lion ate the comedian?
He felt funny.

What do you call a woodpecker with no beak?
A headbanger.

Why can't you play a practical joke on snakes?
Because they don't have a leg to pull.

Why was the bee's hair sticky?
Because he used a honey-comb!

Why did the fish cross the sea?
To get to the other tide.

Why did the chicken cross the road, roll in the mud and cross the road again?
Because it was a dirty double-crosser.

Why did the zookeeper refuse to work in the elephant enclosure?
Because the work kept piling up.

Which side of the chicken has the most feathers?
The outside.

What do you call a sheep in a bikini?
Bra-bra black sheep.

What do you get when you cross a cow with a whale?
Mooby dick.

What's got six legs and can fly long distances?
Three swallows.

Where do Noah's bees live?
In ark hives.

What are teenage giraffes told when they go on their first date?
No necking.

Doctor, Doctor, I feel like a sheep.
That's baaaaaaaaaad!

What's the best way to catch a rabbit?
Hide in the bushes and make a noise like lettuce.

How do you know when a spider is cool?
It has its own website.

What is a polygon?
A dead parrot.

What happens when a chimpanzee sprains his ankle?
He gets a monkey wrench.

What do you get if you cross a tiger with a sheep?
A striped sweater.

What time is it when an elephant climbs into your bed?
Time to get a new bed.

Why did the man cross a chicken with an octopus?
So everyone in his family could have a leg each.

What do you call an amorous insect?
The love bug!

What do you get when you cross a sheep with a radiator?
Central bleating.

Which bird never grows up?
The minor bird.

Are you a vegetarian because you love animals?
No, because I don't like plants.

What do you get when you cross a watch with a parrot?
Politicks.

What language do birds speak?
Pigeon English.

Why is the letter 'T' important to a stick insect?
Because without it, it would be a sick insect.

Why did the fly fly?
Because the spider spied her.

What happened to two frogs that caught the same bug at the same time?
They got tongue-tied.

What is striped and bouncy?
A tiger on a pogo stick.

Why wasn't the butterfly invited to the dance?
Because it was a moth ball.

What do you get if you cross a duck with fireworks?
A fire-quacker.

How do you start a flea race?
One, Two, Flea, Go!

Which animals were the last to leave the ark?
The elephants – they were packing their trunks.

What do elephants take when they can't sleep?
Trunquilisers.

The luckiest bug in the pond

Trouble sleeping? Here.... Take one of these and you'll sleep for a month!

Why don't baby birds smile?
Would you smile if your mother fed you worms all day?

What do you get if you cross a leopard with a watchdog?
A terrified postman.

Which birds steal the soap from the bath?
Robber ducks.

What do parrots eat?
Polyfilla.

What do you get if you cross a parrot with a woodpecker?
A bird that talks in Morse code.

What do you call a mouse that can pick up a monster?
Sir.

What is a termite's favourite breakfast?
Oak-meal.

What do you get if you cross a tiger with a kangaroo?
A striped jumper.

Where did the cow go for its holiday?
Moo Zealand.

Why should you never fight an echidna?
Because she will always win on points.

What are a bee's favourite soap operas?
The Bold & the Bee-utiful and *Days of Our Hives!*

What do you get if you cross a hyena with a bouillon cube?
An animal that makes a laughing stock of itself.

What happened to the horse who swallowed the dollar coin?
He bucked.

What do you get when you cross a master criminal with a fish?
The Codfather.

A pig walks into a bar and asks for a beer.
Bartender: *'That'll be $5. By the way, it's nice to see you. We don't get many pigs in here.'*
Pig: *'At $5 a beer, I'm not surprised.'*

Why did the cat sit on the computer?
To keep an eye on the mouse.

Why was the alligator called Kodak?
Because he was always snapping.

How do dinosaurs pass exams?
With extinction.

Which TV show do cows never miss?
The moos.

Doctor, Doctor, I think I'm a python.
You can't get round me just like that, you know!

What did the termite say when she saw that her friends had completely eaten a chair?
Wooden you know it!

Why did the flies run across the top of the plastic lunch wrap box?
Because it read, 'Tear along the dotted line'.

Where do baby monkeys sleep?
In an apricot.

What do cows listen to?
Moosic.

Which area of the police force accepts monkeys?
The Special Branch.

What do you get if you cross an electric eel with a sponge?
Shock absorbers.

What do you get when you cross a cow with a clairvoyant?
A message from the udder side.

Why were flies playing football in a saucer?
They were playing for the cup.

What do tigers wear in bed?
Striped pyjamas!

Why can't you have a conversation with a goat?
Because it always butts in.

What do you get when you cross a bear with a cow?
Winnie the Moo.

When is a lion not a lion?
When he turns into his den.

How do we know that owls are smarter than chickens?
Have you ever heard of Kentucky-fried owl?

Why are beavers so smart?
Because they gnaw everything.

What is a duck's favourite TV show?
The feather forecast.

When do kangaroos celebrate their birthdays?
During leap year.

SPORT

When fish play football, who is the captain?
The team's kipper!

Coach: *'Our new player cost ten million. I call him our wonder player.'*
Fan: *'Why's that?'*
Coach: *'Every time he plays, I wonder why I bothered to buy him!'*

Coach: *'I'll give you $100 a week to start with, and $500 a week in a year's time.'*
Young player: *'See you in a year!'*

What has twenty-two legs and two wings but can't fly?
A soccer team.

Who won the race between two balls of string?
They were tied!

Why was the boxer known as Picasso?
Because he spent all his time on the canvas.

Why were the arrows nervous?
Because they were all in a quiver.

Why is Cinderella so bad at sport?
Because she has a pumpkin for a coach and she runs away from the ball.

Why is bowling the quietest sport?
Because you can hear a pin drop.

Where do football players dance?
At a football!

What job does Dracula have with the Transylvanian baseball team?
He looks after the bats.

Why does someone who runs marathons make a good student?
Because education pays off in the long run!

Why was the centipede two hours late for the soccer match?
It took him two hours to put his shoes on.

Which goalkeeper can jump higher than a crossbar?
All of them – a crossbar can't jump!

'I can't see us ever finishing this tenpin bowling game.'
'Why is that?'
'Every time I knock all the pins down, someone calls everyone out on strike!'

How do you start a doll's race?
Ready, Teddy, Go!

Why did the soccer star hold his shoe to his ear?
Because he liked sole music!

Why did the footballer take a piece of rope onto the pitch?
He was the skipper!

What part of a football field smells the best?
The scenter spot!

Coach, how would you have played that last shot?
In disguise.

What baseball position did the boy with no arms or legs play?
Home base.

Where do football coaches go when they are sick of the game?
The bored room!

What part of a basketball stadium is never the same?
The changing rooms!

What position did the pile of wood play on the football team?
De-fence!

What happens when baseball players get old?
They go batty.

What are Brazilian soccer fanatics called?
Brazil nuts!

Why did all the bowling pins go down?
Because they were on strike.

Coach, how do I stand for a team trial?
You don't stand, you grovel.

How do hens encourage their favourite basketball teams?
They egg them on!

What are the four seasons?
Baseball, basketball, soccer and football!

Why do artists never win when they play basketball?
They keep drawing the foul!

Why does a polo player ride a horse?
Because they're too heavy to carry.

I've never played so badly.
You mean you've actually played before?

What stories do basketball players tell?
Tall tales!

Why aren't football stadiums built in outer space?
Because there is no atmosphere!

What did one bowling ball say to the other?
Don't stop me, I'm on a roll.

What sort of nails do you find in football shoes?
Toenails.

Why is tennis such a noisy game?
Because everyone raises a racket.

Why is a scrambled egg like a losing team?
They both get beaten.

What did the football player say when he accidentally burped during the game?
Sorry, it was a freak hic!

What did they call Dracula when he won the premiership?
The Champire!

What wears nine gloves, eighteen shoes and a mask?
A baseball team.

Name a tennis player's favourite city.
Volley Wood!

What do you call a cat that plays football?
Puss in boots.

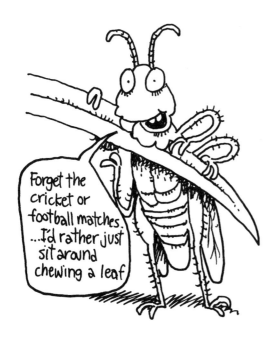

Forget the cricket or football matches ...I'd rather just sit around chewing a leaf

Why don't grasshoppers go to football matches?
They prefer cricket matches!

Where do old bowling balls end up?
In the gutter!

Why didn't the dog want to play football?
It was a boxer!

Why should you be careful when playing against a team of big cats?
They might be cheetahs!

Why wouldn't the coach let elephants on the swim team?
He was afraid they would drop their trunks.

Why are basketball players always so cool?
Because of all the fans.

What does every winner lose in a race?
Their breath.

Why do artists never win when they play football?
They keep drawing!

What happens when an athlete gets angry with his computer?
He becomes a floppy diskus thrower.

I love golf. I could play like this forever.
Don't you want to improve?

Why do football coaches bring suitcases along to away games?
So that they can pack the defence!

I'd like to take it... but I don't think there's room in with my socks

COACH

Coach: *'I thought I told you to lose weight. What happened to your three-week diet?'*

Player: *'I finished it in three days!'*

How did the basketball court get wet?
The players dribbled all over it!

What lights up a football stadium?
A good football game!

Why aren't turkeys allowed to play football?
Because they always use fowl language.

Why was the team manager shaking the cat?
To see if there was any money in the kitty!

What's the smelliest game in the world?
Ping-pong!

Why do soccer players have so much trouble eating?
They think they can't use their hands.

Why did the runner wear rippled sole shoes?
To give the ants a fifty-fifty chance.

Why was the chickens' soccer match a bad idea?
Because there were too many fowls.

What illness do martial artists get?
Kung Flu.

What's a ghost's favourite position in soccer?
Ghoul-keeper.

How do you stop squirrels playing football in the garden?
Hide the ball, it drives them nuts!

MUSIC

What's green and sings?
Elvis Parsley.

What was Pavarotti before he was a tenor?
A niner.

What do you call a small Indian guitar?
A baby sitar.

Did you hear about the silly burglar?
He robbed a music store and stole the lute.

My brother's been practising the violin for ten years.
Is he any good?
No, it was nine years before he found out he wasn't supposed to blow!

What type of music do geologists like best?
Rock.

Where do musicians live?
In A flat.

What shall I sing next?
Do you know 'Bridge Over Troubled Waters?'
Yes.
Then go and jump off it.

Musician 1: *'Who was that piccolo I saw you with last night?'*
Musician 2: *'That was no piccolo. That was my fife.'*

Why couldn't the composer be found?
Because he was Haydn.

I played Beethoven last night?
Who won?

Our Jackie learnt to play the violin in no time at all.
So I can hear.

How many country music singers does it take to change a light bulb?
Two, one to change it, the other to sing about how heartbroken he is that the old one is finished.

Which Christmas song is popular in the Sahara Desert?
O Camel Ye Faithful.

How do you make a bandstand?
Take away their chairs.

My singing teacher said I have voice made in heaven.
No she didn't. She said it was like nothing on earth.

Why was the musician in prison?
Because he was always getting into treble.

What do you call a guy who hangs around musicians?
A drummer.

What kind of music does your father like to sing?
Pop music.

What does a musician take to the supermarket?
A Chopin Lizst.

What do Eskimos sing at birthday parties?
Freeze a Jolly Good Fellow.

This piece of music is haunting.
That's because you're murdering it.

The painful murder of the "1812 Overture"

JOKES ABOUT BOYS

A young boy was helping his dad around the house.

'Son, you're like lightning with that hammer,' said the father.

'Really fast, eh, Dad?' said the boy.

'No, Son. You never strike in the same place twice!'

Boy monster: *'You have a face like a million dollars.'*

Girl monster: *'Have I really?'*

Boy monster: *'Sure, it's green and wrinkly!'*

Did you hear about the little boy who was named after his father?
They called him Dad.

Did you hear about the boy who wanted to run away to the circus?
He ended up in a flea circus!

'Mum, there's a man at the door collecting for the old folks' home,' said the little boy. *'Shall I give him Grandma?'*

'William, I've been told you're fighting with the boys next door and one boy has a black eye,' said his dad.

'Yes Dad,' said William. *'They're twins, and I needed a way to tell them apart!'*

Johnny collected lots of money from trick-or-treating and he went to the store to buy some chocolate.

'You should give that money to charity,' said the shopkeeper.

'No thanks,' replied Johnny. *'I'll buy the chocolate. You give the money to charity!'*

A man whose son had just passed his driving test came home one evening and found that the boy had driven into the living room.

'How did you manage that?' he fumed.

'Quite simple, Dad,' said the boy. *'I just came in through the kitchen and turned left.'*

Why did your brother ask your father to sit in the freezer?
Because he wanted an ice pop!

One day Joe's mother said to his father, *'It's such a nice day, I think I'll take Joe to the zoo.'*
'I wouldn't bother,' said his father.
'If they want him, let them come and get him!'

Dick and Jane were arguing over the breakfast table.
'Oh, you're so stupid!' shouted Dick.
'Dick!' said their father. *'That's quite enough! Now say you're sorry.'*
'Okay,' said Dick. *'Jane, I'm sorry you're stupid.'*

Why was the boy unhappy to win the prize for best costume at the Halloween party?
Because he just came to pick up his little sister!

Igor: *'How was that horror movie you saw last night?'*
Dr Frankenstein: *'Oh, the same old story: Boy meets girl, boy loses girl, boy builds new girl.'*

Ned: *'What does your dad sell?'*
Ed: *'Salt.'*
Ned: *'Well, my dad is a salt seller too.'*
Ed: *'Shake!'*

Little brother: *'Look, Bro, I have a deck of cards.'*
Big brother: *'Big deal!'*

Will and Bill were arguing about whose father was stronger.
Will said, *'Well, you know the Pacific Ocean? My dad dug the hole for it.'*
Bill wasn't impressed.
'Well, that's nothing. You know the Dead Sea? My father's the one who killed it!'

Why did the boy take an aspirin after hearing the werewolf howl?
Because it gave him an eerie ache.

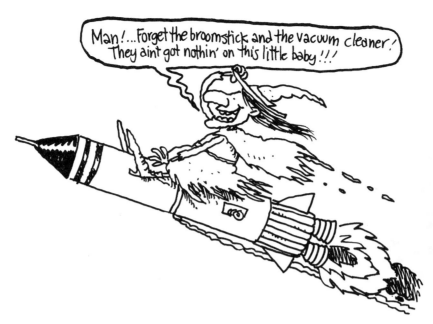

Man !...Forget the broomstick and the vacuum cleaner! They aint got nothin' on this little baby !!!

A boy saw a witch riding on a broomstick.
He asked, *'What are you doing on that?'*
She replied, *'My sister has the vacuum cleaner!'*

'My brother's a professional boxer.'
'Heavyweight?'
'No, featherweight. He tickles his opponents to death!'

Dan: *'My little brother is a real pain.'*
Nan: *'Things could be worse.'*
Dan: *'How?'*
Nan: *'He could be twins!'*

A scoutmaster asked a boy in his troop what good deed he had done that day.
'Well,' said the Scout. *'My Mum only had one chore left, so I let my brother do it.'*

Two boys found themselves in a modern art gallery by mistake.
'Quick,' said one. *'Run, before they say we did it!'*

'Keep that dog out of my garden. It's disgusting!' a neighbour said to a little boy one day.
The boy went home to his family and told them to stay away from the neighbour's garden because of the bad smell!

Why did the boy take a pencil to bed?
To draw the curtains!

I'd tell you another joke about a boy and a pencil, but there's no point.

Good news: Two boys went out to climb trees.
Bad news: One of them fell out.
Good news: A hammock was beneath him.
Bad news: A rake was beside the hammock.
Good news: He missed the rake.
Bad news: He missed the hammock too!

Did you hear about the boy who stole some rhubarb?
He was put into custardy.

Mum: *'How can you practise your trumpet and listen to the radio at the same time?'*
Son: *'Easy, I have two ears!'*

First boy: *'My brother said he'd tell me everything he knows.'*
Second boy: *'He must have been speechless!'*

A little boy came home from his first day at kindergarten and said to his mother, *'What's the use of going to school? I can't read, I can't write and the teacher won't let me talk!'*

Did you hear about the boy who sat under a cow?
He got a pat on the head.

A naughty boy was annoying all the passengers on a plane.
At last, one man could stand it no longer.
'Hey kid,' he shouted. *'Why don't you go outside and play?'*

Did you hear about the carpenter's son?
He was a chip off the old block.

Did you hear about the boy who got worried when his nose grew to be eleven inches long?
He thought it might turn into a foot.

Mum: *'What are you doing, Son?'*
Boy: *'Writing my brother a letter.'*
Mum: *'That's a nice idea, but why are you writing so slowly?'*
Boy: *'Because he can't read very fast!'*

Charley: *'My cat likes to drink lemonade.'*
Lenny: *'He sure must be a sourpuss!'*

A little boy came running into the kitchen.

'Dad, Dad' he said, 'there's a monster at the door with a really ugly face.'

'Tell him you've already got one,' said his father!

Mother: 'Who was that on the phone, Sammy?'

Sammy: 'No one we knew, Mum. Just some man who said it was long distance from India, so I told him I knew that already!'

First boy: 'Why is your brother always flying off the handle?'

Second boy: 'Because he has a screw loose!'

'I think my Dad's getting taller,' said Stan, to his friend.

'What makes you think that?'

'Well, lately I've noticed that his head is sticking through his hair.'

Boys' favourite films: *The Fly*; *Batman*; *Beetlejuice*; *The Sting*; *The Good, the Bug and the Ugly*; *Spawn*; *The Frog Prince*; *Four Webbings and a Funeral*; *Seven Bats for Seven Brothers*.

Two boys camping out in the backyard wanted to know the time, so they started singing at the top of their voices.

Soon, one of the neighbours threw open his window and shouted, 'Hey, cut the noise! Don't you know it's 3 o'clock in the morning?'

'William,' shouted his Mum. 'There were two pieces of cake in that pantry last night, and now there's only one. How do you explain that?'

'It was dark in the pantry,' said William. 'And I didn't see the second piece!'

My boyfriend whispers that he loves me.

Well it's not the sort of thing that he'd admit out loud.

Did you hear about the boy who had to do a project about trains?
He had to keep track of everything.

You can always spot my boyfriend at a party. Look for two people talking, if one looks bored, then the other is my boyfriend.

Did you hear about the boy who was known as Fog?
He was dense and wet!

A boy broke his arm playing football.

After his arm had been put into a cast, he asked the doctor, *'When you take the plaster off, will I be able to play the drums?'*

'Of course you will,' said the doctor, reassuringly.

'That's great!' said the boy. *'I've never been able to play before!'*

What do you get if you cross a zombie with a Boy Scout?
A creature that scares old ladies across the street.

Did you hear about the dizzy Boy Scout?
He spent all day doing good turns.

First witch: *'I took my son to the zoo yesterday.'*
Second witch: *'Really? Did they keep him?'*

Charlie had a puppy on a leash. He met his brother Jim and said, *'I just got this puppy for our little brother.'*
'Really?' said Jim. *'That was a good trade!'*

'Mum, can I please change my name right now?' asked Ben.

'Why would you want to do that, dear?' asked his mum.

'Because Dad says he's going to spank me, as sure as my name's Benjamin!'

Mum: *'Haven't you finished filling the salt shaker yet?'*

Son: *'Not yet. It's really hard to get the salt through all those little holes!'*

A boy staying in an old house meets a ghost in the middle of the night.

'I've been walking these corridors for 300 years,' says the ghost.

'In that case, can you tell me where the bathroom is?' asks the boy.

First boy: *'Does your brother keep himself clean?'*

Second boy: *'Oh, yes. He takes a bath every month, whether he needs one or not!'*

What do you call a boy who is hanging on the wall?
Art!

What do you call a boy who eats his mother and his father?
An orphan.

Mum: *'Why does your little brother jump up and down before taking his medicine?'*

Boy: *'Because he read the label and it said, "Shake well before using".'*

'Why are you crying, Ted?' asked his mum.

'Because my new sneakers hurt,' Ted replied.

'That's because you've put them on the wrong feet.'

'But they're the only feet I have!'

He spent a thousand dollars getting his bad breath cured then found out that no one liked him anyway.

Dad: *'Why is your January progress report so bad?'*

Son: *'Well, you know how it is. Things are always marked down after Christmas!'*

Why did the boy wear five watches?
He liked to have a lot of time on his hands.

Peter: *'My brother wants to work badly!'*

Anita: *'As I remember, he usually does!'*

JOKES ABOUT GIRLS

First witch: *'My, hasn't your little girl grown!'*

Second witch: *'Yes, she's certainly gruesome.'*

Girl: *'Do you like me?'*

Boy: *'As girls go, you're fine – and the sooner you go, the better!'*

Two girls were talking in the corridor.

'That boy over there is getting on my nerves,' said Clare.

'But he's not even looking at you,' replied Megan.

'That's why he's getting on my nerves!' exclaimed Clare.

Mary's class went to the Natural History Museum.

'Did you enjoy yourself?' asked her mother, when she got home.

'Oh, yes,' replied Mary. *'But it was funny going to a dead zoo!'*

First cannibal: *'Who was that girl I saw you with last night?'*

Second cannibal: *'That was no girl. That was my dinner.'*

What is a myth?
A female moth!

'I hope this plane doesn't travel faster than sound,' said the girl to the flight attendant.

'Why?' asked the flight attendant.

'Because my friend and I want to talk, that's why!'

Helen: *'Mum, do you know what I'm going to give you for your birthday?'*

Mum: *'No, dear. What?'*

Helen: *'A nice teapot.'*

Mum: *'But I already have a nice teapot.'*

Helen: *'Not anymore. I just dropped it!'*

What happened to the girl who wore a mouse costume to the Halloween party?
The cat ate her.

BURRRP...!
Oh I hate that synthetic fur!

'Those raisin cookies you sold me yesterday had three cockroaches in them,' a girl complained over the phone, to the baker.

'Sorry about that,' said the baker. 'If you bring the cockroaches back, I'll give you the three raisins I owe you.'

Why did the small werewolf bite the girl's ankle?
Because he couldn't reach any higher.

What do girl snakes write on the bottom of their letters?
With love and hisses!

What did Snow White say while she waited for her photos?
Someday my prints will come!

'What shall we play today?' Tanya asked her best friend Emma.

'Let's play school,' said Emma.

'Okay,' said Tanya. 'But I'm going to be absent.'

Why did Silly Sue throw her guitar away?
Because it had a hole in the middle.

Why did the girl wear a wet shirt all day?
Because the label said 'wash and wear'.

Kate: 'I'm going to cross a galaxy with a frog.'
Sharon: 'You'll be sorry. Don't you know what you'll get?'
Kate: 'No. What?'
Sharon: 'Star warts!'

Sally: 'Can I try on that dress in the window?'
Salesgirl: 'If you like, but most people use the dressing room.'

Have you met the girl who wanted to marry a ghost?
I can't think what possessed her!

Two cannibals were having lunch.
'Your girlfriend makes a great soup,' said one to the other.
'Yes!' agreed the first. 'But I'm going to miss her!'

My sister went on a crash diet.
Is that why she looks a wreck?

Why did the girl give cough syrup to the pony?
Because someone told her it was a little horse.

My sister is so dumb that she thinks a buttress is a female goat!

Why did the wizard turn the naughty girl into a mouse?
Because she ratted on him.

Mother: 'Why did you put a toad in your brother's bed?'
Daughter: 'Because I couldn't find a spider.'

Why was your sister fired from her job as a lift operator?
Because she couldn't remember the route.

First vampire: 'I don't think much of your sister's neck!'
Second vampire: 'Don't worry. Just eat the vegetables.'

Did you hear about the girl monster who wasn't pretty and wasn't ugly?
She was pretty ugly!

What happened when the girl dressed as a spoon left the Halloween party?
No one moved. They couldn't stir without her.

A girl walked into a pet shop and said, 'I'd like a frog for my brother.'
'Sorry,' said the shopkeeper. 'We don't do exchanges!'

So what am I supposed to do now? Hop about wildly all night with a couple of stinky feet?

When you count to 10 using your fingers... Are you allowed to count your thumbs?

What does every girl have that she can always count on?
Fingers.

How did the octopus couple walk down the road?
Arm in arm, in arm, in arm, in arm, in arm, in arm, in arm, in arm ...

Jane: *'Do you ever do any gardening?'*
Wayne: *'Not often. Why?'*
Jane: *'You look as if you could use some remedial weeding.'*

Maria: *'Whatever will Tammy do when she leaves school? She's not smart enough to get a job!'*
Bonnie: *'She could always be a ventriloquist's dummy.'*

James: *'I call my girlfriend Peach.'*
John: *'Because she's soft and beautiful as a peach?'*
James: *'No, because she's got a heart of stone.'*

Why did the girl take a bicycle to bed?
Because she didn't want to walk in her sleep.

Why did the girl plant birdseed?
Because she wanted to raise canaries!

First cannibal: *'My girlfriend's a tough old bird.'*
Second cannibal: *'You should have left her in the oven for another half-hour.'*

Doctor, Doctor, my girlfriend thinks she's a duck.
You'd better bring her in to see me right away.
I can't – she's already flown south for the winter.

Why did the girl have yeast and shoe polish for breakfast?
Because she wanted to rise and shine in the morning!

What happened when the Eskimo girl had a fight with her boyfriend?
She gave him the cold shoulder.

Girl: *'I'd buy that dog, but his legs are too short.'*
Salesgirl: *'Not really. All four of them touch the floor.'*

Why is a bride always out of luck on her wedding day?
Because she never marries the best man.

'Alice, you never get anything right,' complained the teacher. *'What kind of job do you think you'll get when you leave school?'*

'Well, I want to be a weather girl on TV,' said Alice.

What do you call a girl with a frog on her head?
Lily!

What does a girl look for but hopes she'll never find?
A hole in her pantyhose.

Brother: *'Did you just take a shower?'*
Sister: *'Why, is one missing?'*

How many teenage girls does it take to change a light bulb?
One, but she'll be on the phone for five hours telling all her friends about it.

What kind of girl does a mummy take on a date?
Any old girl he can dig up.

Did you hear about the girl who got engaged and then found out her new fiancé had a wooden leg?
She broke it off, of course.

Some girls who are the picture of health are just painted that way.

What did the Eskimo schoolboy say to the Eskimo schoolgirl?
What's an ice girl like you doing in a place like this?

'Are you lost?' the policeman asked the foolish schoolgirl.
'Of course not,' she replied. 'I'm here, it's my school that's lost.'

Did you hear about the girl who was so hung up on road safety that she always wore white at night?
Last winter she was knocked down by a snow plough.

Two girls were having lunch in the schoolyard. One had an apple, and the other said, 'Watch out for worms!'
The first girl replied, 'Why should I? They can watch out for themselves!'

What do young female monsters do at parties?
They go around looking for edible bachelors!

That gorgeous blonde guy is just scrumptious on the pepper crackers!

Penny: 'Will you join me in a cup of hot chocolate?'
Mindy: 'Yes, but do you think we'll both fit?'

Girl to friend: 'I'm sorry, I won't be able to come out tonight. I promised Dad I'd stay in and help him with my homework.'

Mum: 'Jill, go and play with your whistle outside. Your father can't read his paper.'
Jill: 'Wow, I'm only eight and I can read it.'

What did the skeleton say to his girlfriend?
I love every bone in your body!

I can't understand why people say my girlfriend's legs look like matchsticks.
They do look like sticks, but they certainly don't match!

What's small, annoying and really ugly?
I don't know but it comes when I call my sister's name.

Why did the girl cut a hole in her new umbrella?
Because she wanted to tell when it stopped raining!

What kind of sharks never eat women?
Man-eating sharks!

How does a witch doctor ask a girl to dance?
Voodoo like to dance with me?

Lucy: *'If you eat any more ice-cream, you'll burst.'*
Lindy: *'Okay. Pass the ice-cream and duck.'*

Why did the girl jump out of the window?
Because she wanted to try out her new spring suit.

Did you hear about the girl who got her brother a birthday cake but then couldn't figure out how to get the cake in the typewriter to write 'Happy Birthday'?

'My girlfriend says that if I don't give up golf, she'll leave me.'
'Say, that's tough, man.'
'Yeah, I'm going to miss her.'

'It's a pity you've gone on a hunger strike,' said the prisoner's girlfriend on visiting day.
'Why?' asked the prisoner.
'Because I've put a file in your cake!'

First monster: *'That pretty girl over there just rolled her eyes at me.'*
Second monster: *'Well, you'd better roll them back. She might need them!'*

Why doesn't your sister like peanuts?
Have you ever seen a skinny elephant?

As he was walking along a street, the minister saw a little girl trying to reach a high door knocker. Anxious to help, he went over to her. *'Let me do it, dear,'* he said, rapping the knocker. *'Thanks,'* said the little girl. *'Now run like heck!'*

Doctor, Doctor, I think I'm turning into a woman.
Well, you are sixteen now Amanda.

Jane was telling her friend about her holiday in Switzerland. Her friend asked, *'What did you think of the beautiful scenery?'*
'Oh, I couldn't see much,' said Jane. *'There were too many mountains in the way.'*

Why did your sister put her socks on inside out?
Because there was a hole on the outside.

AHHRRR! WHAT'S THAT?
Oh...it's my toe

Biology teacher: *'What kind of birds do we keep in captivity?'*
Janet: *'Jail birds!'*

Mary: *'I've a soft spot for you.'*
Harry: *'Ah, really?'*
Mary: *'Yes, in the middle of a swamp!'*

Why did the girl separate the thread from the needle?
Because the needle had something in its eye.

Boy: *'Dad! Dad! Come out! My sister's fighting a ten-metre gargoyle with three heads!'*
Dad: *'No, I'm not coming out. She's going to have to learn to look after herself.'*

Did you hear about the girl who wrote herself a letter but forgot to sign it?
When it arrived, she didn't know who it was from!

First girl: *'Why are you putting your horse's saddle on backwards?'*
Second girl: *'How do you know which way I'm going?'*

Why didn't the girl want tickets for a door prize?
Because she already had a door.

GHOSTS AND WITCHES

What should you say when you meet a ghost?
How do you boo, sir?

Did you hear about the weather wizard?
He's forecasting sunny spells.

What game do young ghosts love?
Hide and shriek.

What do baby ghosts wear on their feet?
Booties!

What happened to the naughty schoolgirl witch?
She was ex-spelled.

Where do ghosts go to learn to frighten people?
Swooniversity.

What noise does a witch's breakfast cereal make?
Snap, cackle and pop!

Why do ghosts go to parties?
To have a wail of a time.

What's a witch's favourite movie?
Broom with a View.

Who did the witch call when her broom was stolen?
The flying squad.

Why did the witch put her broom in the washing machine?
She wanted a clean sweep!

When do ghosts usually appear?
Just before someone screams!

AAAARRR!

Don't do that! It scares the living daylights out of me

What vehicles race at the Witches' Formula One Grand Prix?
Vroomsticks.

Where do ghosts go swimming?
In the Dead Sea.

What do you call a witch who lives at the beach?
A sand witch!

What do ghosts eat for dinner?
Spook-etti Boo-lognaise.

What is a ghost's favourite dessert?
Boo-berries and I Scream!

Why are ghosts always tired?
Because they are dead on their feet.

What do you call a ghost's mum and dad?
Transparents.

Who is a ghost's favourite singer?
Mighoul Jackson.

What trees do ghosts like best?
Ceme-trees.

Schoolgirl: *'I'm looking for a book called* Ghosts and Ghouls. *Do you know who wrote it?*
Librarian: *'Yes. Sue Pernatural.'*

Did you hear about the ghost who ate all the Christmas decorations?
He got tinselitis.

Why do ghosts hate rain?
It dampens their spirits.

Where do Australian ghosts live?
In the Northern Terror-tory.

Where do ghosts play golf?
At the golf corpse.

What did one ghost say to the other?
Don't spook until you're spooken to!

Why do ghosts speak Latin?
Because it's a dead language.

Did you hear about the ghosts' running race?
It was a dead heat.

Why do witches fly on broomsticks?
Because it's better than walking.

How do you make a witch itch?
Take away the 'w'.

Why couldn't the witch race her horse in the Witches' Derby?
Because it was having a spell.

What kind of mistake does a ghost make?
A boo-boo!

Who is the King of the Wizards?
William the Conjurer.

If you cross a witch's cat with Father Christmas, what do you get?
Santa Claws.

How can you tell what a ghost is getting for its birthday?
By feeling its presence.

What do native American ghosts sleep in?
A creepy teepee!

Why are ghosts cowards?
Because they've got no guts!

What does a ghost have to get before he can scare anyone?
A haunting licence.

What do you call five witches on a broom?
A car pool!

What is a ghost's favourite bedtime story?
Little Boo Peep!

What do witches put in their hair?
Scare spray.

What is a witch's favourite class in school?
Spelling!

What do ghosts do to keep fit?
They hire an exercisist.

What do ghosts use to type letters?
A type-frighter.

Hold onto your hats girls while I try to turn this old stick into a stretch limo

He's not stupid; he's possessed by a foolish ghost.

What do you call the ghost of a chicken?
A poultrygeist.

What did the skeleton say to the twin witches?
Which witch is which?

Where do ghosts live?
On dead ends!

What does a ghost do when he gets in a car?
Puts his sheet belt on!

How many witches does it take to change a light bulb?
Just one, but she changes it into a frog!

What is a spook's favourite ride?
A rollerghoster!

What do you call a witch without a broomstick?
A witch-hiker.

What do you get when a ghost sits in a tree?
Petrified wood!

Why did the witches go on strike?
Because they wanted sweeping reforms.

What do you get if you cross Bambi with a ghost?
Bamboo.

Why do ghosts like the Spice Girls?
Because they're an all ghoul band.

What do you do if you're surrounded by a witch, a werewolf, a vampire and two ghosts?
Hope you're at a fancy dress party.

What do you get if you cross a ghost with a packet of nuts?
Snacks that go crunch in the night!

A ghost walks into a bar.
Bartender: *'Sorry, we don't serve spirits here.'*

What kind of witch turns out the lights?
A Light-witch!

Why are ghosts such terrible liars?
Because you can see right through them.

Why didn't the ghost eat liver?
He didn't have the stomach for it!

What story do little witches like to hear at bedtime?
Ghoul deluxe and the three scares!

What do you call a motor bike belonging to a witch?
A brooooooooooom stick!

What do ghosts eat for breakfast?
Dreaded wheat!

What was the wizard's favourite band?
ABBA-cadabra.

Why do witches get good bargains?
Because they're good at haggling.

How do you know when a ghost is sad?
He says Boooooooooo Hooooooooo!

What did the mother ghost say to the baby ghost?
Put your boos and shocks on!

What is a ghost's favourite type of fruit?
Boo-berry!

What do you get when you cross a heater with a witch?
A hot spell.

How does a witch tell the time?
With a witch watch!

Which ghost is President of France?
Charles de Ghoul.

What did the wizard say to his witch girlfriend?
Hello, gore-juice!

What do you call two witches that share a room?
Broom mates!

Who speaks at the ghosts' press conference?
The spooksperson!

What do little ghosts play with?
Deady bears.

FABULOUS FOOD

Waiter, how did this fly get in my soup?
I guess it flew.

Waiter, remove this fly now.
But he hasn't finished yet.

Waiter, there's a fly on my steak.
That's because it's attracted to rotting meat.

What's small, round, white and giggles?
A tickled onion.

Which cheese is made backwards?
Edam.

What is a goal keeper's favourite snack?
Beans on post!

Two turkeys walk into a bar.
Barman: *'Sorry, we don't serve food in here.'*

How do you make a cream puff?
Make it run around the block.

What is the difference between a hungry person and a greedy person?
One longs to eat, and the other eats too long.

Why did the lazy boy get a job in a bakery?
Because he wanted a good loaf!

Waiter, I'd like burnt steak and soggy chips with a grimy, bitter salad.
I'm afraid the chef won't cook that for you, sir.
Why not? He did yesterday.

What did the banana sitting in the sun say to the other banana sitting in the sun?
I don't know about you but I'm starting to peel.

How can you tell the difference between a can of soup and a can of baked beans?
Read the label.

Waiter, this soup tastes funny.
Why aren't you laughing then?

What is a cannibal's favourite soup?
One with a lot of body.

Waiter, this egg is bad.
Well don't blame me, I only laid the table.

What's the difference between a marshmallow and a pykost?
What's a pykost?
About two dollars.

Waiter, is this beef or lamb?
Can't you taste the difference?
No.
Then it doesn't matter.

What's a lawyer's favourite dessert?
Suet.

Why do gingerbread men wear trousers?
Because they have crummy legs.

What's too scared to be eaten?
Chicken soup.

A punch-up at the Punch Bowl

How do you make a fruit punch?
Give it boxing lessons.

What's rhubarb?
Embarrassed celery.

Waiter, we'll have two coffees please. And I want a clean cup.
Yes sir. … Here are your two coffees. Now which one of you wanted the clean cup?

Why is a psychiatrist like a squirrel?
Because he's surrounded by nuts.

Waiter, there's a fly in my soup.
Yes sir, the hot water killed it.

Have you heard the joke about the butter?
I better not tell you, you might spread it.

Why did the baby cookie cry?
Because his mother was a wafer so long.

Why did the potato cry?
Because the chips were down.

Waiter, I'm in a hurry. Will my pizza be long?
No, it will be round.

What do you call a fake noodle?
An impasta.

What do you get when you cross a baby rabbit with a vegetable?
A bunion.

How do you start a race between two rice puddings?
Sago.

Bob...the lazier of the two rice puddings was down on his training so kept losing his spoon ... then lagged behind at the finish, which eventually lost him the pudding race.

Waiter, I'll have the soup and the fish please.

I would recommend you eat the fish first. It's been sitting around for a few days and is starting to smell.

Why do watermelons get married?
Because they can't-elope.

What do you call an egg in the jungle?
An eggsplorer.

Waiter, there's a fly in my soup.
No sir, that's a cockroach. The fly's on your roll.

What do you call two rows of vegetables?
A dual cabbageway.

How do you make a strawberry shake?
Tell it a scary story.

Why did the balloon burst?
Because it saw a lolly pop.

Why did the jelly wobble?
Because it saw the apple turnover.

What did one tomato say to the other that was behind him?
Ketchup!

Mum, can I have a dollar for the man who's crying in the park?
What's he crying about?
He's crying, 'Hot dogs one dollar.'

Where do bakers keep their dough?
In the bank.

What has bread on both sides and is afraid of everything?
A chicken sandwich.

Waiter, there's a fly in my soup!
Don't worry sir, the spider in your salad will get it!

Waiter, bring me something to eat and make it snappy?
How about an alligator sandwich, sir?

What flies and wobbles?
A jellycopter.

Waiter there's a fly in my soup.
Well you did order fly soup, ma'am.

What are two things you cannot have for breakfast?
Lunch and dinner.

How do you make an apple crumble?
Smash it with a mallet.

Waiter, do you have frogs' legs?
No, I've always walked like this.

Waiter, I can't eat this meal. Fetch me the manager.
It's no use. He won't eat it either.

What vegetable can you play snooker with?
A cue-cumber.

Hey! There's no chicken in this chicken pot pie.
Well do you expect to find dogs in dog biscuits?

ERRRRRR! That's not the sort of Apple Crumble I was thinking of!

What's the difference between packed lunches and a pile of slugs?
Packed lunches are in boxes.

What happened when there was a fight in the fish and chip shop?
Two fish got battered.

When the cannibal crossed the Pacific on a cruise ship, he told the waiter to take the menu away and bring him the passenger list!

Doctor, Doctor, my wife thinks I'm crazy because I like sausages.
That's ridiculous. I like sausages too.
Good, you should come round and see my collection some time. I've got hundreds of them.

Waiter, there's a fly in my soup.
Would you prefer him in your main course?

What jam can't you eat?
A traffic jam!

Why does steak taste better in space?
Because it is meteor.

What do fishermen eat at Easter?
Oyster eggs.

How do you make a Swiss roll?
Push him down a hill.

Waiter, what kind of soup is this?
Bean soup.
I don't care what it's been. What is it now?

Why don't nuts go out at night?
Because they don't want to be assaulted.

Why should you never tell secrets in a grocery store?
Because the corn has ears, potatoes have eyes and beanstalk.

What's the difference between pea soup and roast chicken?
Anyone can roast chicken.

Why is a pea small and green?
If it was large and red it would be a fire engine.

Why don't eggs tell jokes?
They'd crack each other up!

What happened to the male bee who fell in love?
He got stuck on his honey.

Waiter, what's this in my soup?
I don't know, sir. All bugs look the same to me.

Waiter, this crab has only got one claw.
It must have been in a fight.
Then bring me the winner.

How do you fix a broken pizza?
With tomato paste.

Can I have an ice-cream for my little boy?
I'd prefer it if you gave me money.

What's the best way to face a timid mouse?
Lie down in front of its mouse hole and cover your nose with cheese spread!

Doctor, Doctor, I feel like an apple.
We must get to the core of this!

Waiter, your finger is in my bowl of soup.
Don't worry. The soup isn't hot.

A mushroom walks into a bar and says to the bartender, *'Get me a drink!'* But the bartender refuses. The mushroom says, *'Why not? I'm a fungi!'*

What's the difference between a young lady and a fresh loaf?
One is a well-bred maid and the other is well-made bread.

Waiter, I'll have the burger please.
With pleasure.
No, with fries.

Waiter, there's a dead fly swimming in my soup.
There can't be, sir. Dead flies can't swim.

The cruise-ship passenger was feeling really seasick, when the waiter asked if he'd like some lunch.
'No thanks,' he replied. *'Just throw it over the side and save me the trouble.'*

What's yellow and square?
A tomato in disguise.

What did the mayonnaise say to the fridge?
Close the door, I'm dressing.

Waiter, this coffee tastes like mud.
I can't understand why. It was ground just a minute ago.

How do you make an elephant sandwich?
Well first you take an enormous loaf of bread…

Johnny, I think your dog likes me, he's been looking at me all night.
That's because you're eating out of his bowl.

What did the raspberry say to the other raspberry?
We shouldn't have got into this jam.

Why did the fool get fired from the banana factory?
He threw out all the bent ones.

If I had six grapefruit in one hand and seven in the other what would I have?
Very big hands.

What's a lion's favourite food?
Baked beings.

What do lions say before they go out hunting for food?
Let us prey.

What vegetable goes well with jacket potatoes?
Button mushrooms.

Waiter, do you have frogs' legs?
Yes sir.
Then hop into the kitchen and fetch me a steak.

Waiter, is there any soup on the menu?
No madam, I've wiped it all off.

How do you make a potato puff?
Chase it around the garden.

Waiter, what is this fly doing in my soup?
Freestyle I believe.

What did the computer say to the programmer at lunchtime?
Can I have a byte?

How do you make a French fry?
Leave him in the sun.

What do nudists like to eat best?
Skinless sausages.

Waiter, there's a spider in my soup.
It must have eaten the fly.

Why did the raisin go out with the prune?
Because he couldn't find a date.

Why did the man at the orange juice factory lose his job?
He couldn't concentrate!

What's long and green and slowly turns red?
A cucumber holding its breath.

Doctor, Doctor, should I surf the Internet on an empty stomach?
No, you should do it on a computer.

Waiter, there's a flea in my soup.
Tell him to hop it.

Waiter, there's a cockroach in my soup.
Sorry sir, we're all out of flies.

Girl: *'How much is a soft drink?'*
Waitress: *'Fifty cents.'*
Girl: *'How much is a refill?'*
Waitress: *'The first is free.'*
Girl: *'Well then, I'll have a refill.'*

Amy: *'Did you find your cat?'*
Karen: *'Yes, he was in the refrigerator.'*
Amy: *'Goodness, is he okay?'*
Karen: *'He's more than okay – he's a cool cat!'*

What has ears but cannot hear?
A field of corn.

Why do little brothers chew with their mouths full?
Flies have got to live somewhere.

Waiter, I'll have the lamb chops. And make them lean.
Certainly sir. To the right or the left?

Mummy, Mummy, Daddy's on fire!
Hurry up and get the marshmallows.

Mummy, Mummy, can I lick the bowl?
No! You'll have to flush like everyone else.

What are coloured sprinkles?
M&M poo.

What's yellow and smells of bananas?
Monkey vomit.

What's red, white and brown, and travels faster than the speed of sound?
An astronaut's ham and tomato sandwich.

Why did the tomato blush?
Because it saw the salad dressing.

Waiter, there's a fly in my soup.
That's because the chef used to be a tailor.

Mummy, Mummy, I can't find the dog's food.
Shut up and eat your stew.

Why do toadstools grow so close together?
They don't need mushroom.

Waiter, there's a fly in my soup.
I find that hard to believe sir. The chef used them all in the casserole.

What has eyes but cannot see?
A potato.

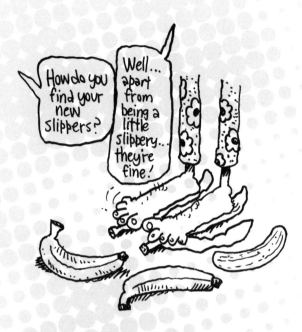

What do you call banana skins that you wear on your feet?
Slippers.

If olive oil is made from olives and peanut oil is made from peanuts, what is baby oil made from?

Doctor, Doctor, I dreamed that I ate a large marshmallow!
Did you wake up without a pillow?

What's red and goes up and down?
A tomato in a lift.

What can you serve but never eat?
A volleyball.

On what nuts can pictures hang?
Walnuts.

If you have a referee in football, what do you have in bowls?
Cornflakes.

What do computers do when they get hungry?
They eat chips.

Doctor, Doctor, I keep thinking I'm a fruitcake.
What's got into you?
Flour, raisins and cherries.

If a butcher is two metres tall and has size 11 feet, what does he weigh?
Meat.

Waiter, what do you call this dish?
Chicken surprise.
But I can't see any chicken.
That's the surprise.

Just HEAT and SERVE ...umm that's quick and easy!

TINNED KNIGHT

What did the dragon say when he saw the knight in his shining armour?
Oh no! Not more canned food!

What are monsters' favourite lunches?
Shepherds Pie and Ploughmans Lunch.

Where do sharks shop?
The fish market.

How do you make a banana split?
Cut it in half.

What happened when the fool couldn't tell the difference between porridge and putty?
All his windows fell out.

What did the cat have for breakfast?
Mice bubbles.

Waiter, you've got your thumb on my steak!
Well I didn't want to drop it again.

What was the best thing before sliced bread?

What do you get from nervous cows?
Milk shakes.

What do cows eat for breakfast?
Mooslie.

How do you fix a cracked pumpkin?
With a pumpkin patch.

What do you get when you cross an orange with a squash court?
Orange squash.

Waiter, this apple pie is squashed.
Well you told me to step on it because you were in a hurry.

Why did the elephant paint the bottom of his feet yellow?
So he could hide upside down in custard.

Why was the elephant standing on the marshmallow?
He didn't want to fall in the hot chocolate.

What's yellow, brown and hairy?
Cheese on toast dropped on the carpet.

What is big, green and has a trunk?
An unripe elephant.

What do frogs order in restaurants?
French Flies!

Where do ants eat?
A restaur-ant.

What did the lioness say to the cub chasing the hunter?
Stop playing with your food.

What's the best way to catch a monkey?
Climb a tree and act like a banana.

What do patriotic American monkeys wave on July 4?
Star spangled bananas.

Where does a pig go to pawn his watch?
A ham hock shop.

FAMILY FUN

The mother monster asked her son what he was doing with a saw, and if he'd seen his brother.

'You mean my new half-brother, Mummy,' he replied!

Why was the baby pen crying?
Because its mum was doing a long sentence.

I just got a bunch of flowers for my wife.

Great swap.

What's old, wrinkled and hangs out your underwear?
Your Grandma.

What do you call the cannibal who ate her father's sister?
An aunt-eater!

My cousin spent heaps on deodorant, until he found out people just didn't like him.

Uncle Hubert noticed that his nephew Johnny was watching him the whole time.

'Why are you always looking at me?' he asked.

'I was just wondering when you were going to do your trick,' replied Johnny.

'What trick?' asked Uncle Hubert.

'Well, Mum says you drink like a fish…'

A woman was facing court, charged with wounding her husband.

'You're very lucky you're not facing a murder charge – why did you stab him over a hundred times?' asked the judge.

'I didn't know how to turn off the electric carving knife,' she replied.

Mother: *'Cathy, get your little sister's hat out of that puddle!'*
Cathy: *'I can't, Mum. She's got it strapped too tight under her chin.'*

Mummy, Mummy, I don't want to go to New Zealand.
Shut up and keep swimming.

Mummy, Mummy, Dad has been run over by a steamroller.
Shut up and slide him under the door.

Mummy, Mummy, are you sure you bake bread this way?
Shut up and get back in. I can't close the oven door.

Mummy, Mummy, I've just chopped my foot off.
Then hop out of the kitchen, I've just mopped the floor.

Little brother: *'I'm going to buy a sea horse.'*
Big brother: *'Why?'*
Little brother: *'Because I want to play water polo!'*

My dad once stopped a man ill-treating a donkey. It was a case of brotherly love.

Mummy, Mummy, why can't we buy a garbage disposal unit?
Shut up and keep chewing.

Mummy, Mummy, Daddy's hammering on the roof again.
Shut up and drive a bit faster.

Doctor, Doctor, my brother thinks he's a chicken.
How long has this been going on?
About six months.
Why didn't you bring him here earlier?
We needed the eggs.

Doctor, Doctor, my sister thinks she's a squirrel.
Sounds like a nut case to me.

Doctor, Doctor, my son swallowed a pen, what should I do?
Use a pencil instead!

'Can I go swimming now, Mum?' asked the child.
'No – there are sharks at this beach,' said his mother.
'Dad's swimming!'
'Yes, he's got a million dollars' life insurance…'

Mum, Mum, Dad's broken my computer!
How did he do that?
I dropped it on his head!

Doctor, Doctor, my baby's swallowed some explosives.
Well, don't annoy him. We don't want him to go off.

Doctor, Doctor, my little brother thinks he's a computer.
Well, bring him in so I can cure him.
I can't, I need to use him to finish my homework!

Doctor, Doctor, my little boy has just swallowed a roll of film.
Hmmm. Let's hope nothing develops!

Doctor, Doctor, my husband smells like a fish.
Poor sole!

What did the little light bulb say to its mum?
I wuv you watts and watts.

Doctor, Doctor, my sister thinks she's a lift.
Well, tell her to come in.
I can't, she doesn't stop at this floor!

Doctor, Doctor, my wife keeps beating me.
Oh dear. How often?
Every time we play Scrabble.

Father: *'Johnny got an A on his assignment! I think he got his brains from me.'*
Mother: *'I think you're right. I've still got mine.'*

Doctor, Doctor, my wife's contractions are only five minutes apart.
Is this her first child?
No, this is her husband.

Doctor, Doctor, my sister keeps thinking she's invisible.
Which sister?

What's the definition of minimum?
A very small mother.

TOTALLY RANDOM

What do you do with crude oil?
Teach it some manners.

Why does the Statue of Liberty stand in New York Harbour?
Because it can't sit down.

What do you get when an elephant stands on your roof?
Mushed rooms.

Davey: *'Dad, there's a man at the door collecting for a new swimming pool.'*
Dad: *'Alright, give him a glass of water.'*

One Sunday morning, a little old lady saw a boy walking through the park carrying a fishing pole and a jar of tadpoles.

'Young man,' she said. *'You shouldn't be going fishing on a Sunday!'*

'I'm not going fishing, Ma'am,' he called back. *'I'm going home!'*

What looks like Blu-Tack, feels like Blu-Tack, tastes like Blu-Tack, but isn't Blu-Tack?
Smurf poo.

What's a sick joke?
Something that comes up in conversation.

What do you call a boy with really short hair?
Sean!

A woman woke her husband in the middle of the night.

'There's a burglar in the kitchen eating the cake I made this morning!' she said.

'Who should I call?' asked her husband. *'The police or an ambulance?'*

When the silly man's co-worker asked why he had a sausage stuck behind his ear, he replied, *'Oh – I must have eaten my pencil for lunch!'*

All I've got is two dried beans and a mouldy lump of bread

Why did Robin Hood rob the rich?
The poor didn't have any money.

What do you give an elephant with diarrhoea?
Plenty of room.

A man out for a walk came across a little boy pulling his cat's tail.

'Hey you!' he shouted. *'Don't pull the cat's tail!'*

'I'm not pulling,' replied the boy. *'I'm only holding on – the cat's doing the pulling!'*

Three guys, Shutup, Manners and Poop, drove too fast and Poop fell out of the car.

Shutup went to the police station, where the policeman asked, *'What's your name?'*

'Shutup,' he answered.
'Hey – where are your manners!' the policeman exclaimed.

Shutup replied, *'Outside on the road, scrapin' up Poop!'*

George knocked on the door of his friend's house.

When his friend's mother answered he asked, *'Can Albert come out to play?'*

'No,' said Albert's mother. *'It's too cold.'*

'Well then,' said George, *'can his football come out to play?'*

What do Eskimos get from sitting on the ice too long?
Polaroids.

Mummy, Mummy, my head hurts.
Shut up and get away from the dartboard.

Doctor, Doctor, my stomach is sore.
Stop your bellyaching.

Doctor, Doctor, I've spent so long at my computer that I now see double.
Well, walk around with one eye shut.

Why are cooks mean?
Because they beat the eggs and whip the cream!

O.k. you guys... let's get it straight from the start as to who's boss around here

CREAM

Doctor, Doctor, I'm suffering from hallucinations.
I'm sure you are only imagining it.

Doctor, Doctor, nobody ever listens to me.
Next!

Doctor, Doctor, what does this X-ray of my head show?
Unfortunately nothing.

Doctor, Doctor, I accidentally ate my pillow!
Don't be so down in the mouth.

A boy was on a full subway, when a heavy woman next to him said, *'If you were a gentleman, you'd stand up and let someone else sit down.'*
The boy replied, *'And if you were a lady, you'd stand up and let four people sit down.'*

Doctor, Doctor, everyone hates me.
Don't be stupid, not everyone has met you yet.

Doctor, Doctor, everyone thinks I'm a liar.
I don't believe you.

Doctor, Doctor, I have yellow teeth, what should I do?
Wear a brown tie.

Doctor, Doctor, I'm as sick as a dog.
Well, I can't help you because I'm not a vet.

Doctor, Doctor, I keep thinking I'm a dog.
How long has this been going on?
Ever since I was a pup.

Doctor, Doctor, my hair is falling out, can you give me something to keep it in?
Yes, a paper bag.

Now listen here Sonny-boy. If you were any sort of gentleman you'd use that crow bar and get me out of this seat!

Oh...no thanks! That cherry looks fattening!

A fat man went into a café and ordered two slices of apple pie with four scoops of ice-cream, covered with whipped cream and piled high with chopped nuts.

'Would you like a cherry on top?' asked the waitress.

'No thanks,' said the man. *'I'm on a diet.'*

Doctor, Doctor, I think I've been bitten by a vampire.

Drink this glass of water.

Will it make me better?

No, but I'll be able to see if your neck leaks!

Doctor, Doctor, I have a sore throat.

Pull your pants down and put your backside against the window.

What's that got to do with my sore throat?

Nothing. I just hate my neighbours.

Doctor, Doctor, my little boy swallowed a bullet, what should I do?

Well for a start, don't point him at me.

Doctor, Doctor, have you taken my temperature?

No. Is it missing?

Doctor, Doctor, I keep seeing an insect spinning.

Don't worry, it's just a bug that's going around.

Doctor, Doctor, I need some acetylsalicylic acid.

You mean aspirin?

That's it. I can never remember that word.

Doctor, Doctor, I keep thinking I'm a billiard ball.

Well, get back in the queue.

How do you sink a submarine full of fools?
Knock on the door.

What happened to the stupid jellyfish?
It set.

Three girls walked into a beauty salon. Two had blonde hair and one had green hair. The stylist asked the blondes, *'How did you get to be blonde?'*

'Oh, it's natural,' they replied.

The stylist asked the other girl, *'How did your hair become green?'*

She replied, *'Rub your hand on your nose and then across your hair.'*

Doctor, Doctor, I feel like a bird.
I'll tweet you in a minute.

Doctor, Doctor, I've been turned into a hare!
Stop rabbiting on about it.

Doctor, Doctor, my tongue tingles when I touch it to an unsalted peanut wrapped in used toaster oven aluminium foil. What's wrong with me?
You have far too much free time.

Doctor, Doctor, I think I'm an adder.
Great, can you help me with my accounts then please?

Doctor, Doctor, how much to have this splinter pulled out?
Seventy dollars.
Seventy dollars for just a couple of minutes' work?
I can pull it out very slowly if you like.

Doctor, Doctor, I keep thinking I'm a mosquito.
Go away, sucker!

Doctor, Doctor, I get very nervous and frightened during driving tests.
Don't worry, you'll pass eventually.
But I'm the examiner!

Sam: *'Mum, can I have a pony for Christmas?'*

Mum: *'Of course not. You'll have turkey just like the rest of us.'*

Doctor, Doctor, I think I'm losing my mind.
Don't worry, you won't miss it.

Doctor, Doctor, I was playing a kazoo and I swallowed it.
Lucky you weren't playing the piano.

Hey Doc... I didn't swallow my kazoo... ...it was in my pocket all along!

Doctor, Doctor, my baby looks just like his father.

Never mind – just as long as he's healthy.

What do you call a man with a spade?
Doug.

What do you call a woman in the distance?
Dot!

What do you call a man with a plank on his head?
Edward.

What do you call a man with a crane on his head?
Derek!

What do you call a man with a wig on his head?
Aaron!

What do you call a man with a mat on his head?
Neil!

What do you call a woman with a radiator on her head?
Anita!

What do you call a woman with slates on her head?
Ruth!

What do you call a man with a stamp on his head?
Frank!

Doctor, Doctor, I feel like an apple.
Well don't worry, I won't bite.

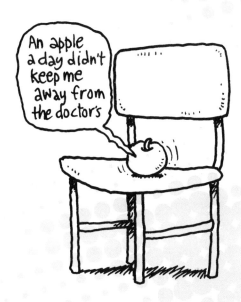

What do you call a woman with two toilets on her head?
Lulu!

What do you call a woman with a twig on her head?
Hazel!

What do you call a man with a kilt on his head?
Scott!

What do you call a man with a truck on his head?
The deceased!

A man came running out of his house as the garbage truck was driving by.

Man: *'Did I miss the garbage collection?'*

Garbage man: *'No, jump in.'*

What stays hot in the fridge?
Mustard.

What do you call a boy who is always getting up your nose?
Vic!

What do you call a man with beef, gravy and vegetables on his head?
Stu!

Why did the cleaning woman quit?
Because grime doesn't pay.

Why was the computer in pain?
It had a slipped disk!

What kind of car did Elvis drive?
A Rock-n-Rolls Royce.

Why did the computer sneeze?
It had a virus.

The secret to making great wine... dirty feet

What do you get when you step on a grape?
A little wine.

How can you tell when a fool has been using the computer?
There is correction fluid all over the screen!

Doctor, Doctor, I've broken my arm in two places.
Well, don't go back there again.

What nut is like a sneeze?
A cashew.

Doctor, Doctor, I think I'm a yo-yo.
You're stringing me along!

Doctor, Doctor, I tend to flush a lot.
Don't worry, it's just a chain reaction.

What do you get when you cross a skunk with Frankenstein?
Stinkenstein!

Why did the lizard cross the road?
To see his flat mate.

What swings through the trees and is very dangerous?
A chimpanzee with a machine gun.

John: *'Have you noticed your mother smells a bit funny these days?'*
Will: *'No. Why?'*
John: *'Well, your sister told me she was giving her a bottle of toilet water for her birthday!'*

Do you think it's a cold coming on?

What did the teddy bear say when he was offered dessert?
No thanks, I'm stuffed!

Why was the computer so tired when it got home?
Because… it had a hard drive!

Doctor, Doctor, everyone thinks I'm a liar.
Well, that's hard to believe!

Why was the fool's brain the size of a pea after exercising?
It swelled up!

Waiter, there's a bug in my soup.
Be quiet sir or everyone will want one.

Why was the fool covered in bruises?
He started to walk through a revolving door and then changed his mind!

How do you make a fool laugh on a Sunday?
Tell him a joke on Saturday.

What did the foolish ghost do?
Climbed over walls.

How do you make a Venetian blind?
Put a blind fold on him.

What do you get if you cross a computer programmer with an athlete?
A floppy diskus thrower.

What is the difference between a fool and a shopping cart?
A shopping cart has a mind of its own.

When is a car not a car?
When it turns into a garage.

What holds the moon up?
Moonbeams!

What did the metric alien say?
Take me to your litre!

How do spacemen pass the time on long trips?
They play astronauts and crosses!

How do you get a baby astronaut to sleep?
You rock-et!

What do you call a pretty and friendly witch?
A failure.

What do you call a man with a map on his head?
Miles.

Why are naughty kids like maggots?
Because they try to wriggle out of everything.

The TRAIN went this way....

How can you find a lost train?
Follow its tracks.

Customer: *'I cleaned my computer, and now it doesn't work.'*
Repairman: *'What did you clean it with?'*
Customer: *'Soap and water.'*
Repairman: *'Water's not meant to be used on a computer!'*
Customer: *'Oh, I bet it wasn't the water that caused the problem. It was when I put it in the dryer!'*

Brother: *'What happened to you?'*
Sister: *'I fell off while I was riding.'*
Brother: *'Horseback?'*
Sister: *'I don't know. I'll find out when I get back to the stable.'*

What do you get when you cross a football player with a gorilla?
I don't know but nobody tries to stop it from scoring.

Your kids just seem to wriggle out of everything!

I know they do. They're just like their father! I met him wiggling out of a trashcan!

What did the mosquito say when he saw a camel's hump?
Gee, did I do that?

Why did the computer cross the road?
Because it was programmed by the chicken.

What do baby swans dance to?
Cygnet-ure tunes.

Did you here about the bungee jumper who shot up and down for three hours before they could bring him under control?
He had a yo-yo in his pocket!

When George left school he was going to be a printer. All his teachers said he was the right type.

What is the computer's favourite dance?
Disk-o.

What bet can never be won?
The alphabet.

Which of the witches' friends eats the fastest?
The goblin.

What has two hands, no fingers, stands still and runs?
A clock.

Did you hear about the little spook who couldn't sleep at night because his brother kept telling him human stories?

What flies around all day but never goes anywhere?
A flag.

Why did the singer climb a ladder?
To reach the high notes.

What is always coming but never arrives?
Tomorrow.

What's green, has eight legs and would kill you if it fell on you from out of a tree?
A billiard table.

What can't walk but can run?
A river.

If a horse loses its tail, where could it get another?
At a re-tail store.

How does a fireplace feel?
Grate!

What feature do witches love on their computers?
The spell-checker.

What aftershave do monsters prefer?
Brute.

When Adam introduced himself to Eve, what three words did he use which read the same, backwards and forwards?
Madam, I'm Adam.

Why were the boy's photos not ready when he called for them?
The photographer was a late developer.

What do you draw without a pencil or paper?
A window shade.

What goes around the house and in the house but never touches the house?
The sun.

Waiter there is a small insect in my soup!
Sorry sir, I'll get you a bigger one!

Do they sterilise needles for lethal injections?

Why did the girl keep a ruler on her newspaper?
Because she wanted to get the story straight.

What do you make from baked beans and onions?
Tear gas.

What do you call a ship that lies on the bottom of the ocean and shakes?
A nervous wreck.

What did the tie say to the hat?
You go on ahead, I'll just hang around.

What did the pencil sharpener say to the pencil?
Stop going in circles and get to the point!

How do you make holy water?
You burn the hell out of it.

What makes you seasick?
Your little brother's vomit.

What did the didgeridoo?
Answered the phone when the boomerang.

What did the first mind reader say to the second mind reader?
You're all right, how am I?

Three tourists were driving down the highway trying to get to Disneyland. They saw a sign that read 'Disneyland Left'. So they went home.

Did you hear about the fool who paid five dollars to have his thoughts read?
He got his money back.

How can you tell when a moth farts?
He flies straight for a second.

How many programmers does it take to screw in a light bulb?
None, it's a hardware problem!

What did the traffic light say to the car?
Don't look now, I'm changing.

What do you give a sick car?
A fuel injection.

Waiter, how long will my sausages be?
Oh, about eight centimetres.

Two sausages are in a pan. One looks at the other and says, *'Gosh, it's hot in here,'* and the other sausage says, *'GOODNESS GRACIOUS, IT'S A TALKING SAUSAGE!'*

Policeman: *Did you know that you were driving at 190 km/h?*
Driver: *Impossible. I've only been in the car for five minutes.*

There's no point in telling some people a joke with a double meaning. They wouldn't understand either of them!

John: *'Do you know anyone who has gone on the television?'*
Wendy: *'Just my dog, but he's housetrained now.'*

Woops! nicked a hydraulic oil line

How does a robot alien shave?
With a laser blade!

Where do chickens go when they die?
To oven.

Why did the boy become an astronaut?
Because he had his head in the stars.

How do you know when there is an elephant in the fridge?
There are footprints in the butter.

Do you turn on your computer with your left hand or your right hand?
My right hand.
Amazing! Most people have to use the on/off switch!

Why was the computer so thin?
Because it hadn't had many bytes!

What's the difference between a buffalo and a bison?
You can't wash your hands in a buffalo.

Brother: *'Where was Solomon's temple?'*
Sister: *'On either side of his head.'*

I've been on my computer all night!
Don't you think you'd be more comfortable on a bed, like everyone else?

What happened to the wooden car with wooden wheels and a wooden engine?
It wooden go!

What do you call a space magician?
A flying sorcerer!

THE GREATEST MAGIC SHOW IN THE UNIVERSE!

If everyone bought a white car, what would we have?
A white carnation.

How does a witch make scrambled eggs?
She holds the pan and gets two friends to make the stove shake with fright.

Is that the computer help line? Every time I log on to the Seven Dwarfs website, my computer screen goes snow white...

What did the mother shrimp say to her baby when they saw a submarine?
Don't be scared – it's only a can of people.

Why did the golfer wear two pairs of pants?
In case he got a hole in one.

FOUR!

How many pairs of pants are you wearing?

Even basketballers start off by dribbling

When is a baby like a basketball player?
When he dribbles.

Why did the ghost go to jail?
For driving without due scare and attention.

Why is a ladies' belt like a garbage truck?
Because it goes around and around, and gathers the waist.

What's red and white?
Pink.

What colour is a hiccup?
Burple.

Why are giraffes good friends to have?
Because they stick their neck out for you.

My kids are just a bunch of dim 5 Watt-ers

Why was the glow-worm unhappy?
Her children weren't very bright.

What did the big chimney say to the little chimney?
You're too young to smoke.

What did the big telephone say to the little telephone?
You're too young to get engaged.

How do fishermen make a net?
They make lots of holes and tie them together with string.

When do mathematicians die?
When their number is up.

What did the ground say to the rain?
If this keeps up, I'll be mud.

How many animals did Moses fit in the Ark?
None, it was Noah's Ark.

How did Noah steer the Ark at night?
He switched on the floodlights.

Where was Noah when the lights went out?
In d'ark.

How did the Vikings send messages?
By Norse code.

What has two legs and two tails?
A lizard flipping a coin.

Your dog is so slow, he brings in last week's newspaper.

What instrument does a fisherman play?
A cast-a-net.

Your feet are so smelly, your shoes refuse to come out of the closet.

I'd leave you with one thought if you had somewhere to put it.

What's green and slimy and hangs from trees?
Giraffe boogie.

What's big and white and can't jump over a fence?
A fridge.

How do computers make cardigans?
On the interknit.

What did the beaver say to the tree?
It's been nice gnawing you.

What do ghosts do in the January sales?
Go bargain haunting.

What's thick and black and picks its nose?
Crude oil.

I bought this computer yesterday and I found a twig in the disk drive!
I'm sorry, sir. You'll have to speak to the branch manager.

Did you hear about the monkey who left bits of his lunch all over the computer?
His dad went bananas.

I want to be an astronaut when I grow up.
What high hopes you have!

What do you call an expensive car with a cheap name?
A poor-sche.

Where are computers kept at school?
On their floppy desks.

When is a chair like a woman's dress?
When it's satin.

Why did the fool go in the ditch?
Her turn signal was on.

Visitor: *'You're very quiet, Louise.'*
Louise: *'Well, my mum gave me a dollar not to say any thing about your red nose.'*

What's the difference between a maggot and a cockroach?
Cockroaches crunch more when you eat them.

How many clothing shop assistants does it take to change a light bulb?
Three, one to change it, one to say how well it fits and one to say that the colour is perfect.

What kind of song can you sing in the car?
A cartoon (car tune)!

What do you call the bugs on the moon?
Luna-tics.

Where are English kings and queens crowned?
On the head.

Who invented the weekend?
Robinson Crusoe – he had all his work done by Friday.

Did you hear about the criminal contortionist?
He turned himself in.

Did you hear about the unlucky sailor?
First he was shipwrecked, then he was rescued – by the *Titanic*.

What happened when the bell fell in the swimming pool?
It got wringing wet.

Where do musical frogs perform?
At the Hopera House.

The police are looking for a monster with one eye. They should use two!

Why did the criminals whisper in the meadow?
Because they didn't want to be overheard by the grass.

Who's faster than a speeding bullet and full of food?
Super Market.

Which song is top of the Eskimo hit parade?
'There's No Business Like Snow Business'.

What is the difference between a bus driver and a cold?
One knows the stops, the other stops the nose.

I'm really more the BIKINI ON A BEACHTOWEL sort of girl myself...

Why do skeletons hate winter?
Because the cold goes right to their bones!

Why do bagpipers walk when they play?
They're trying to get away from the noise.

What goes in pink and comes out blue?
A swimmer on a cold day!

Small monster: *'Dad, the dentist wasn't painless like he said he'd be.'*
Dad monster: *'Did he hurt you?'*
Small monster: *'No, but he yelled when I bit his finger!'*

Did you hear the joke about the fart?
It stinks.

Mummy, Mummy, Daddy just put Rover down.
I'm sure he had a good reason for it.
But he promised I could do it.

How do you get four suits for a couple of dollars?
Buy a pack of cards.

What did the dentist want?
The tooth, the whole tooth and nothing but the tooth.

What do you get when two prams collide?
A creche.

What did the shoe say to the foot?
You're having me on.

Why can't a bicycle stand up?
Because it's two tyred.

LAZY BONES!

KNOCK KNOCK

Knock Knock. *Who's there?*
Abbey! *Abbey who?*
Abbey hive is where honey is made!

Knock Knock. *Who's there?*
Kim! *Kim who?*
Kim too late by the look of it!

Knock Knock. *Who's there?*
Boo! *Boo who?*
What are you crying about?

Knock Knock. *Who's there?*
Bat! *Bat who?*
Bat you'll never guess!

Knock Knock. *Who's there?*
Wooden shoe! *Wooden shoe who?*
Wooden shoe like to know!

Knock Knock. *Who's there?*
Eight! *Eight who?*
Eight my lunch too quickly!
Now I've got a stomach ache!

Knock Knock. *Who's there?*
Accordion! *Accordion who?*
Accordion to the TV, it's going to rain
tomorrow!

Knock Knock. *Who's there?*
Beth! *Beth who?*
Beth wisheth, thweetie!

Knock Knock. *Who's there?*
Cameron! *Cameron who?*
Cameron a flash are what you need
to take pictures in the dark!

Who's the new Dutch boy down the end
between the Italian girl and the Aussie rubber thong

Knock Knock. *Who's there?*
Celia! *Celia who?*
Celia later alligator!

Knock Knock. *Who's there?*
Cosi! *Cosi who?*
Cosi had to!

Knock Knock. *Who's there?*
Manny! *Manny who?*
Manny are called, few are chosen!

Knock Knock. *Who's there?*
Diesel! *Diesel who?*
Diesel help with your cold! Take two every four hours!

Knock Knock. *Who's there?*
Ahmed! *Ahmed who?*
Ahmed a mistake! I think I want the house next door!

Knock Knock. *Who's there?*
Evan! *Evan who?*
Evan you should know who I am!

Knock Knock. *Who's there?*
Flea! *Flea who?*
Flea thirty is when I've got to be home!

Knock Knock. *Who's there?*
Fozzie! *Fozzie who?*
Fozzie hundredth time, my name is Nick!

Knock Knock. *Who's there?*
Germaine! *Germaine who?*
Germaine you don't recognise me?

Knock Knock. *Who's there?*
Guinea! *Guinea who?*
Guinea some money so I can buy some food!

Knock Knock. *Who's there?*
Hacienda! *Hacienda who?*
Hacienda the story! It's bedtime now!

Knock Knock. *Who's there?*
Lass! *Lass who?*
Are you a cowboy?

Knock Knock. *Who's there?*
House! *House who?*
House it going?

Knock Knock. *Who's there?*
Irish stew! *Irish stew who?*
Irish stew in the name of the law!

Knock Knock. *Who's there?*
Gizza! *Gizza who?*
Gizza kiss!

Knock Knock. *Who's there?*
Ines! *Ines who?*
Ines second I'm going to turn around and go home!

Knock Knock. *Who's there?*
Jam! *Jam who?*
Jam mind, I'm trying to get out!

Knock Knock. *Who's there?*
Jean! *Jean who?*
Jean-ius! Ask me a question!

Knock Knock. *Who's there?*
Adore! *Adore who?*
Adore is for knocking on!

kissy kissy kissy

Left over right....
no...right over left
...right behind the left one
left...

Knock Knock. *Who's there?*
Waiter. *Waiter who?*
Waiter minute while I tie my shoe.

Knock Knock. *Who's there?*
Knee! *Knee who?*
Knee-d you ask?

Knock Knock. *Who's there?*
Kent! *Kent who?*
Kent you let me in?

Knock Knock. *Who's there?*
Leonie! *Leonie who?*
Leonie one for me!

Knock Knock. *Who's there?*
Midas! *Midas who?*
Midas well let me in!

Knock Knock. *Who's there?*
Cecil! *Cecil who?*
Cecil have music where ever she goes!

Knock Knock. *Who's there?*
Moira! *Moira who?*
The Moira merrier!

Knock Knock. *Who's there?*
Nero! *Nero who?*
Nero far!

Knock Knock. *Who's there?*
Nobody! *Nobody who?*
Just nobody!

Knock Knock. *Who's there?*
Jaws! *Jaws who?*
Jaws truly!

Knock Knock. *Who's there?*
Iran! *Iran who?*
Iran ten laps around the track and I'm very tired now!

Knock Knock. *Who's there?*
Neil! *Neil who?*
Neil down and take a look through the letter slot!

Knock Knock. *Who's there?*
Oboe! *Oboe who?*
Oboe, I've got the wrong house!

Knock Knock. *Who's there?*
Onya! *Onya who?*
Onya marks, get set, go!

Knock Knock. *Who's there?*
P! *P who?*
(shouts) P nuts, P nuts, get your fresh P nuts!

Knock Knock. *Who's there?*
Pa! *Pa who?*
Pa-don me! Can I come in?

Knock Knock. *Who's there?*
Sigrid! *Sigrid who?*
Sigrid Service, now do exactly as I say!

Knock Knock. *Who's there?*
Paula! *Paula who?*
Paula nother one! It's got bells on it!

Knock Knock. *Who's there?*
Pinza! *Pinza who?*
Pinza needles!

Knock Knock! *Who's there?*
Irish! *Irish who?*
Irish I knew some more Knock Knock jokes.

Ahhr... to be shur...to be shur...
Ay cairnt think of one
more knock-knock joke

Knock Knock. *Who's there?*
Renata! *Renata who?*
Renata milk, can you spare a cup?

Knock Knock. *Who's there?*
Who! *Who who?*
What are you – an owl?

Knock Knock. *Who's there?*
Radio! *Radio who?*
Radio not, here I come!

Knock Knock. *Who's there?*
Rhoda! *Rhoda who?*
(sings) Row, Row, Rhoda boat!

Knock Knock. *Who's there?*
The Sultan! *The Sultan who?*
The Sultan Pepper!

Knock Knock. *Who's there?*
Justin! *Justin who?*
Justin time for lunch!

Knock Knock. *Who's there?*
Sal! *Sal who?*
Sal long way for me to go home!

Knock Knock. *Who's there?*
Shirley! *Shirley who?*
Shirley you know by now!

Knock Knock. *Who's there?*
Paul! *Paul who?*
Paul thing! Let me in and I'll comfort you!

Knock Knock. *Who's there?*
Snow! *Snow who?*
Snow good asking me!

Knock Knock. *Who's there?*
Mister! *Mister who?*
Mister last train home!

Knock Knock. *Who's there?*
Stan! *Stan who?*
Stan back! I'm going to break the door down!

Knock Knock. *Who's there?*
Tex! *Tex who?*
Tex two to tango!

Knock Knock. *Who's there?*
Alota! *Alota who?*
Alota good this is doing me!

Knock Knock. *Who's there?*
Tom Sawyer! *Tom Sawyer who?*
Tom Sawyer skipping school!

Knock Knock. *Who's there?*
Poker! *Poker who?*
Poker and see if she'll wake up!

Knock Knock. *Who's there?*
William! *William who?*
William mind your own business?

Knock Knock. *Who's there?*
Rocky! *Rocky who?*
Rocky bye baby on the tree top!

Knock Knock. *Who's there?*
Watson! *Watson who?*
Watson TV tonight?

Knock Knock. *Who's there?*
Police! *Police who?*
Police let me in!

Knock Knock. *Who's there?*
Panther! *Panther who?*
My panther falling down!

Knock Knock. *Who's there?*
Bear! *Bear who?*
Bearer of glad tidings!

Knock Knock. *Who's there?*
Avon! *Avon who?*
Avon you to be my wife!

Knock Knock. *Who's there?*
Wenceslas! *Wenceslas who?*
Wenceslas bus home?

Knock Knock. *Who's there?*
Aesop! *Aesop who?*
Aesop I saw a puddy cat!

Knock Knock. *Who's there?*
Tish! *Tish who?*
Bless you!

Knock Knock. *Who's there?*
Alex! *Alex who?*
Alexplain later, just let me in!

Knock Knock. *Who's there?*
Joan! *Joan who?*
Joan call us, we'll call you!

Knock Knock. *Who's there?*
Armageddon! *Armageddon who?*
Armageddon out of here!

Knock Knock. *Who's there?*
Arncha! *Arncha who?*
Arncha going to let me in? It's freezing out here!

Knock Knock. *Who's there?*
Bab! *Bab who?*
Baboons are a type of ape!

Knock Knock. *Who's there?*
Razor! *Razor who?*
Razor hands, this is a stick up!

Knock Knock. *Who's there?*
Bean! *Bean who?*
Bean working too hard lately!

Knock Knock. *Who's there?*
Bing! *Bing who?*
Bingo starts in half an hour!

Knock Knock. *Who's there?*
Ammonia! *Ammonia who?*
Ammonia little girl who can't reach the doorbell!

Knock Knock. *Who's there?*
Arch! *Arch who?*
Bless you!

Knock Knock. *Who's there?*
Butcher! *Butcher who?*
Butcher hand on the doorknob and let me in!

Knock Knock. *Who's there?*
Betty! *Betty who?*
Betty let me in or there'll be trouble!

Knock Knock. *Who's there?*
Noah! *Noah who?*
Noah yes? What's your decision?

Knock Knock. *Who's there?*
Beth! *Beth who?*
Bethlehem is where Jesus was born!

BUTCHER LEFT LEG IN AND SHAKE IT ALL ABOUT

Knock Knock. *Who's there?*
Butcher! *Butcher who?*
Butcher left leg in, butcher left leg out…

Knock Knock. *Who's there?*
Carrie! *Carrie who?*
Carrie on with what you're doing!

Knock Knock. *Who's there?*
C-2! *C-2 who?*
C-2 it that you remember me next time!

Knock Knock. *Who's there?*
Curry! *Curry who?*
Curry me back home please!

Knock Knock. *Who's there?*
Dingo! *Dingo who?*
Dingo anywhere on the weekend.

Knock Knock. *Who's there?*
Costas! *Costas who?*
Costas a fortune to make the trip here!

Knock Knock. *Who's there?*
Wanda! *Wanda who?*
Wanda buy some cookies?

Knock Knock. *Who's there?*
Cattle! *Cattle who?*
Cattle always purr when you stroke it!

Knock Knock. *Who's there?*
Moppet! *Moppet who?*
Moppet up before someone slips!

Knock Knock. *Who's there?*
Closure! *Closure who?*
Closure mouth when you're eating!

Knock Knock. *Who's there?*
Doris! *Doris who?*
The Doris locked so let me in!

Knock Knock. *Who's there?*
Eddie! *Eddie who?*
Eddie body home?

Knock Knock. *Who's there?*
Ears! *Ears who?*
Ears some more knock knock jokes!

Knock Knock. *Who's there?*
Fantasy! *Fantasy who?*
Fantasy a walk on the beach?

Knock Knock. *Who's there?*
Europe! *Europe who?*
Europen the door so I can come in!

Knock Knock. *Who's there?*
Bacon! *Bacon who?*
Bacon a cake for your birthday!

Knock Knock. *Who's there?*
Caesar! *Caesar who?*
Caesar quickly, before she gets away!

Knock Knock. *Who's there?*
Eye! *Eye who?*
Eye know who you are! Don't you know who I am?

Knock Knock. *Who's there?*
Foster! *Foster who?*
Foster than a speeding bullet!

Knock Knock. *Who's there?*
Frank! *Frank who?*
Frankly my dear, I don't give a damn!

Knock Knock. *Who's there?*
Canoe! *Canoe who?*
Canoe come out and play with me?

Knock Knock. *Who's there?*
Harmony! *Harmony who?*
Harmony electricians does it take to change a light bulb?

Knock Knock. *Who's there?*
Ima! *Ima who?*
Ima going to home if you don't let me in!

Knock Knock. *Who's there?*
Gus! *Gus who?*
No, you guess who. I already know!

Knock Knock. *Who's there?*
Howdy! *Howdy who?*
Howdy do that?

Knock Knock. *Who's there?*
Grant! *Grant who?*
Grant you three wishes!

Knock Knock. *Who's there?*
Germany! *Germany who?*
Germany people knock on your door?

Knock Knock. *Who's there?*
Haden! *Haden who?*
Haden seek!

Knock Knock. *Who's there?*
Hammond! *Hammond who?*
Hammond eggs for breakfast please!

Knock Knock. *Who's there?*
Smore! *Smore who?*
Can I have smore marshmallows?

Knock Knock. *Who's there?*
Felix! *Felix who?*
Felix my ice-cream I'll lick his!

Knock Knock. *Who's there?*
Kanga! *Kanga who?*
No, kangaroo!

Knock Knock. *Who's there?*
Augusta! *Augusta who?*
Augusta wind blew my hat away!

Knock Knock. *Who's there?*
Lee King! *Lee King who?*
Lee King bucket!

Knock Knock! *Who's there?*
Max! *Max who?*
Max no difference who it is – just open the door!

Knock Knock. *Who's there?*
Les! *Les who?*
Les go out for dinner!

Knock Knock. *Who's there?*
Lon! *Lon who?*
Lon ago, in a land far, far away…

Knock Knock. *Who's there?*
Harlow! *Harlow who?*
Harlow Dolly!

Knock Knock. *Who's there?*
Minnie! *Minnie who?*
Minnie people would like to know!

Knock Knock. *Who's there?*
Jim! *Jim who?*
Jim mind if we come in!

Knock Knock. *Who's there?*
Luke! *Luke who?*
Luke through the peephole and you'll see!

Knock Knock. *Who's there?*
Mayonnaise! *Mayonnaise who?*
Mayonnaise are hurting! I think I need glasses!

Knock Knock. *Who's there?*
Colin! *Colin who?*
Colin all cars! Colin all cars!

Knock Knock. *Who's there?*
Nest! *Nest who?*
Nest time I'm going to ring before I come!

Knock Knock. *Who's there?*
Ooze! *Ooze who?*
Ooze in charge around here!

Knock Knock. *Who's there?*
Bassoon! *Bassoon who?*
Bassoon things will be better!

Knock Knock. *Who's there?*
Norway! *Norway who?*
Norway am I leaving until I've spoken to you!

Knock Knock. *Who's there?*
Nobody! *Nobody who?*
No body, just a skeleton!

Knock Knock. *Who's there?*
Olive! *Olive who?*
Olive in that house across the road!

Knock Knock. *Who's there?*
Olga! *Olga who?*
Olga way if you don't let me in!

Knock Knock. *Who's there?*
Parish! *Parish who?*
Parish is the capital of France!

Knock Knock. *Who's there?*
Packer! *Packer who?*
Packer your troubles in your old kit bag!

Knock Knock. *Who's there?*
Phil! *Phil who?*
Phil my glass up to the rim!

Knock Knock. *Who's there?*
Quacker! *Quacker who?*
Quacker 'nother bad joke and I'm leaving!

Knock Knock. *Who's there?*
Ringo! *Ringo who?*
Ringo, Ringo roses!

Knock Knock. *Who's there?*
Lionel! *Lionel who?*
Lionel bite you if you don't watch out!

Knock Knock. *Who's there?*
Miniature! *Miniature who?*
Miniature let me in I'll tell you!

Knock Knock. *Who's there?*
Russell! *Russell who?*
Russell up something to eat please!

Knock Knock. *Who's there?*
Bashful! *Bashful who?*
I'm too shy to tell you!

Knock Knock. *Who's there?*
Roxanne! *Roxanne who?*
Roxanne pebbles are all over your garden!

Knock Knock. *Who's there?*
Nanna! *Nanna who?*
Nanna your business!

Knock Knock. *Who's there?*
Shelby! *Shelby who?*
Shelby comin' round the mountain when she comes!

Knock Knock! *Who's there?*
Stopwatch! *Stopwatch who?*
Stopwatch you're doing and open this door!

Knock Knock. *Who's there?*
Sabina! *Sabina who?*
Sabina long time since I've been at your place!

Knock Knock. *Who's there?*
Hey! *Hey who?*
Hey ho, hey ho, it's off to work we go!

Knock Knock. *Who's there?*
Sharon! *Sharon who?*
Sharon share alike!

Knock Knock. *Who's there?*
Barry! *Barry who?*
Barry the treasure where no one will find it!

Knock Knock. *Who's there?*
Tank! *Tank who?*
You're welcome!

Knock Knock. *Who's there?*
Theresa! *Theresa who?*
Theresa green!

Knock Knock. *Who's there?*
Teresa! *Teresa who?*
Teresa green, the sky is blue!

Knock Knock. *Who's there?*
Tex! *Tex who?*
Tex one to know one!

Knock Knock. *Who's there?*
Voodoo! *Voodoo who?*
Voodoo you think you are?

Knock Knock. *Who's there?*
Toucan! *Toucan who?*
Toucan play at this game!

Knock Knock. *Who's there?*
Una! *Una who?*
No I don't, tell me!

Knock Knock. *Who's there?*
Wicked! *Wicked who?*
Wicked be a great couple if you gave me a chance!

Knock Knock. *Who's there?*
Robin! *Robin who?*
Robin you, so hand over your cash!

Knock Knock. *Who's there?*
Sombrero! *Sombrero who?*
(sings) Sombrero-ver the rainbow!

Knock Knock. *Who's there?*
Water! *Water who?*
Water friends for!

Knock Knock. *Who's there?*
Tommy! *Tommy who?*
Tommy you love me!

Knock Knock. *Who's there?*
Carlotta! *Carlotta who?*
Carlotta trouble when it breaks down!

Knock Knock. *Who's there?*
Xavier! *Xavier who?*
Xavier breath, I'm not leaving!

Knock Knock. *Who's there?*
Avenue! *Avenue who?*
Avenue heard these jokes before?

Knock Knock. *Who's there?*
Yah! *Yah who?*
Ride 'em cowboy!

Knock Knock. *Who's there?*
Zany! *Zany who?*
Zany body home?

Knock Knock. *Who's there?*
Amiss! *Amiss who?*
Amiss you! That's why I'm here!

Knock Knock. *Who's there?*
Alison! *Alison who?*
Alison to the radio!

Knock Knock. *Who's there?*
Xena! *Xena who?*
Xena minute!

Knock Knock. *Who's there?*
Alaska! *Alaska who?*
Alaska one more time. Let me in!

Knock Knock. *Who's there?*
Abbot! *Abbot who?*
Abbot you don't know who this is!

Knock Knock. *Who's there?*
Baby Owl! *Baby Owl who?*
Baby Owl see you later, maybe
I won't!

Knock Knock. *Who's there?*
Troy! *Troy who?*
Troy as I may I can't reach the bell!

Knock Knock. *Who's there?*
Abel! *Abel who?*
Abel seaman!

Knock Knock. *Who's there?*
Fang! *Fang who?*
Fangs for opening the door!

Knock Knock. *Who's there?*
Adder! *Adder who?*
Adder you get in here?

Knock Knock. *Who's there?*
Abyssinia! *Abyssinia who?*
Abyssinia when I get back!

Knock Knock. *Who's there?*
Banana! *Banana who?*
Banana split, so ice-creamed!

Knock Knock. *Who's there?*
Sarah! *Sarah who?*
Sarah doctor in the house? I don't feel so good!

Knock Knock. *Who's there?*
Beck! *Beck who?*
Beckfast is ready!

Knock Knock. *Who's there?*
Witches! *Witches who?*
Witches the way home?

Come on baby start...!

Knock Knock. *Who's there?*
Abbey! *Abbey who?*
Abbey stung me on the nose!

Knock Knock. *Who's there?*
Beet! *Beet who?*
Beets me! I've forgotten my own name!

Knock Knock. *Who's there?*
Diego! *Diego who?*
Diegos before the B!

Knock Knock. *Who's there?*
Bea! *Bea who?*
Because I said so!

Knock Knock. *Who's there?*
Catch! *Catch who?*
God bless you!

Knock Knock. *Who's there?*
Butcher! *Butcher who?*
Butcher money where your mouth is!

Knock Knock. *Who's there?*
Bach! *Bach who?*
Bach of chips!

Knock Knock. *Who's there?*
Ellie! *Ellie who?*
Ellie-phants never forget!

Knock Knock. *Who's there?*
Burglar! *Burglar who?*
Burglars don't knock!

Knock Knock. *Who's there?*
Butcher! *Butcher who?*
Butcher arms around me!

Knock Knock. *Who's there?*
Adair! *Adair who?*
Adair once, but I'm bald now!

Knock Knock. *Who's there?*
Cornflakes! *Cornflakes who?*
I'll tell you tomorrow, it's a cereal!

Knock Knock. *Who's there?*
Chuck! *Chuck who?*
Chuck if I've left my keys inside!

Knock Knock. *Who's there?*
Cologne! *Cologne who?*
Cologne me names won't get you anywhere!

Knock Knock. *Who's there?*
Beezer. *Beezer who?*
Beezer black and yellow and make honey.

Knock Knock. *Who's there?*
Carrie! *Carrie who?*
Carrie me inside, I'm exhausted!

Knock Knock. *Who's there?*
Hans! *Hans who?*
Hans are on the ends of your arms!

Knock Knock. *Who's there?*
Cash! *Cash who?*
Are you a nut?

Knock Knock. *Who's there?*
Caesar! *Caesar who?*
Caesar jolly good fellow!

Knock Knock. *Who's there?*
Beef! *Beef who?*
Bee fair now!

Knock Knock. *Who's there?*
Dat! *Dat who?*
Dat's all folks!

Knock Knock. *Who's there?*
Dale! *Dale who?*
Dale come if you ask dem!

Knock Knock. *Who's there?*
Byra! *Byra who?*
Byra light of the silvery moon!

Knock Knock. *Who's there?*
Disguise! *Disguise who?*
Disguise the limit!

Knock, Knock. *Who's there?*
Weed. *Weed who?*
Weed better mow the lawn before it gets too long.

Knock Knock. *Who's there?*
Turnip. *Turnip who?*
Turnip for school tomorrow or there will be trouble.

Knock Knock. *Who's there?*
Dan! *Dan who?*
Dan Druff!

Knock Knock. *Who's there?*
Eiffel! *Eiffel who?*
Eiffel down!

Knock Knock. *Who's there?*
Brie! *Brie who?*
Brie me my supper!

Knock Knock. *Who's there?*
Eugene! *Eugene who?*
Eugene, me Tarzan!

Knock Knock. *Who's there?*
Despair! *Despair who?*
Despair tyre is flat!

Knock Knock. *Who's there?*
Figs! *Figs who?*
Figs the doorbell, it's been broken for ages!

Knock Knock. *Who's there?*
Gwen! *Gwen who?*
Gwen will I see you again?

Knock Knock. *Who's there?*
Cow goes! *Cow goes who?*
Cow goes 'moo', not 'who'!

Knock Knock. *Who's there?*
Owl goes! *Owl goes who?*
That's right, owl goes who!

Knock Knock. *Who's there?*
Fly! *Fly who?*
Fly away Peter, fly away Paul!

Knock Knock. *Who's there?*
Alan! *Alan who?*
Alan a good cause!

Knock Knock. *Who's there?*
Gary! *Gary who?*
Gary on smiling!

Knock Knock. *Who's there?*
Gorilla! *Gorilla who?*
Gorilla cheese sandwich for me, please!

Knock Knock. *Who's there?*
Freeze! *Freeze who?*
Freeze a jolly good fellow!

Knock Knock. *Who's there?*
Howard! *Howard who?*
Howard I know?

Knock Knock. *Who's there?*
Hair! *Hair who?*
I'm hair to stay!

Knock Knock. *Who's there?*
Carmen! *Carmen who?*
Carmen get it!

Knock Knock. *Who's there?*
Heidi! *Heidi who?*
Heidi ho!

Knock Knock. *Who's there?*
Ice-cream! *Ice-cream who?*
Ice-cream, you scream!

Knock Knock. *Who's there?*
Icy! *Icy who?*
I see your underwear!

Knock Knock. *Who's there?*
Ida! *Ida who?*
Ida hard time getting here!

Knock Knock. *Who's there?*
Ivan! *Ivan who?*
No, Ivanhoe!

Knock Knock. *Who's there?*
Lillian! *Lillian who?*
Lillian the garden!

Knock Knock. *Who's there?*
Knock Knock. *Who's there?*
Knock Knock. *Who's there?*
I'm sorry, but Mum told me never to speak to strangers.

Knock Knock. *Who's there?*
Ice-cream soda. *Ice-cream soda who?*
Ice-cream soda neighbours wake up!

Knock Knock. *Who's there?*
Ivor! *Ivor who?*
Ivor you let me in or I'll break the door down!

Knock Knock. *Who's there?*
Jamaica! *Jamaica who?*
Jamaica mistake!

Knock Knock. *Who's there?*
Jilly! *Jilly who?*
Jilly out here, so let me in!

Knock Knock. *Who's there?*
Meg! *Meg who?*
Meg up your own mind!

Knock Knock. *Who's there?*
Juan! *Juan who?*
Juan to come out and play?

Knock Knock. *Who's there?*
Juno! *Juno who?*
I know who, Juno who?

Knock Knock. *Who's there?*
Jo! *Jo who?*
Jo jump in the lake!

Knock Knock. *Who's there?*
Aida! *Aida who?*
Aida whole box of chocolates and now I feel sick!

Knock Knock. *Who's there?*
Jewell! *Jewell who?*
Jewell know me when you see me!

Knock Knock. *Who's there?*
Letter. *Letter who?*
Letter in or she'll knock the door down.

Knock Knock. *Who's there?*
Kareem! *Kareem who?*
Kareem rises to the surface!

Knock Knock. *Who's there?*
Lauren! *Lauren who?*
Lauren order!

Knock Knock. *Who's there?*
Hijack! *Hijack who?*
Hi Jack! Where's Jill?

Knock Knock. *Who's there?*
Lois! *Lois who?*
Lois the opposite of high!

Knock Knock. *Who's there?*
Larva! *Larva who?*
I larva you!

Knock Knock. *Who's there?*
May! *May who?*
Maybe I'll tell you, maybe I won't!

Knock Knock. *Who's there?*
Mira! *Mira who?*
Mira, Mira on the wall!

Knock Knock. *Who's there?*
Lena! *Lena who?*
Lena little closer and I'll tell you!

Knock Knock. *Who's there?*
Zombies. *Zombies who?*
Zombies make honey, zombies just buzz around.

Knock Knock. *Who's there?*
Wayne. *Wayne who?*
Wayne, Wayne, go away, come again
another day!

Knock Knock. *Who's there?*
Mary! *Mary who?*
Mary Christmas and a happy new
year!

Knock Knock. *Who's there?*
Matt! *Matt who?*
Matter of fact!

Knock Knock. *Who's there?*
Jess! *Jess who?*
Jess me and my shadow!

Knock Knock. *Who's there?*
Mabel! *Mabel who?*
Mabel doesn't work either!

Knock Knock. *Who's there?*
Noah! *Noah who?*
Noah good place for a meal?

Knock Knock. *Who's there?*
Nobel! *Nobel who?*
No bell so I just knocked!

Knock Knock. *Who's there?*
Orson! *Orson who?*
Orson cart!

Knock Knock. *Who's there?*
Avenue! *Avenue who?*
Avenue got a doorbell?

Knock Knock. *Who's there?*
Jasmine! *Jasmine who?*
Jasmine play the saxophone, piano
and trumpet!

Knock Knock. *Who's there?*
Olivia! *Olivia who?*
Olivia but I've lost my key!

Knock Knock. *Who's there?*
Oil! *Oil who?*
Oil be seeing you!

Knock Knock. *Who's there?*
Ocelot! *Ocelot who?*
Ocelot of questions, don't you?

Knock Knock. *Who's there?*
Pier! *Pier who?*
Pier through the peephole and you'll see!

Knock Knock. *Who's there?*
Tuba! *Tuba who?*
Tuba toothpaste!

Knock Knock. *Who's there?*
Patrick! *Patrick who?*
Patricked me into coming over!

Knock Knock. *Who's there?*
Roach! *Roach who?*
Roach out, I'll be there!

Knock Knock. *Who's there?*
Pecan! *Pecan who?*
Pecan someone your own size!

Knock Knock. *Who's there?*
Oppa! *Oppa who?*
Oppa-tunity knocks!

Knock Knock. *Who's there?*
Mary Lee. *Mary Lee who?*
Mary Lee, Mary Lee, Mary Lee, Mary Lee, Life is but a dream.

YODEL-A-EE-OOO

Knock Knock. *Who's there?*
Little old lady. *Little old lady who?*
I didn't know you could yodel!

Knock Knock. *Who's there?*
Raoul! *Raoul who?*
Raoul with the punches!

Knock Knock. *Who's there?*
Pa! *Pa who?*
Pa-tridge in a pear tree!

Knock Knock. *Who's there?*
Rosa! *Rosa who?*
Rosa my favourite flowers!

Knock Knock. *Who's there?*
Ralph! *Ralph who?*
Ralph! Ralph! Ralph! I'm a dog!

Knock Knock. *Who's there?*
Rose! *Rose who?*
Rose early to come and see you!

Knock Knock. *Who's there?*
Scott! *Scott who?*
Scott nothing to do with you!

Knock Knock. *Who's there?*
Still! *Still who?*
Still knocking!

Knock Knock. *Who's there?*
U-! *U- who?*
U for me and me for you!

Knock Knock. *Who's there?*
Eliza. *Eliza who?*
Eliza wake at night thinking about you.

Eliza wake thinking about you all night...every night!

Knock Knock. *Who's there?*
Justice! *Justice who?*
Justice I thought! You won't let me in!

Knock Knock. *Who's there?*
Sacha! *Sacha who?*
Sacha fuss you're making!

Knock Knock. *Who's there?*
Tick! *Tick who?*
Tick 'em up, I'm a tongue-tied towboy!

Knock Knock. *Who's there?*
Says! *Says who?*
Says me!

Knock Knock. *Who's there?*
Dewayne! *Dewayne who?*
Dewayne the bathtub before I drown!

Knock Knock. *Who's there?*
Satin! *Satin who?*
Who satin my chair!

Knock Knock. *Who's there?*
Sam! *Sam who?*
Sam person who knocked a minute ago!

Knock Knock. *Who's there?*
Sibyl! *Sibyl who?*
Sibyl Simon met a pieman going to the fair!

Knock Knock. *Who's there?*
Spell! *Spell who?*
W!H!O!

Knock Knock. *Who's there?*
Havana! *Havana who?*
Havana great time!

Knock Knock. *Who's there?*
Red! *Red who?*
Knock Knock. *Who's there?*
Red! *Red who?*
Knock Knock. *Who's there?*
Red! *Red who?*
Knock Knock. *Who's there?*
Red! *Red who?*
Knock Knock. *Who's there?*
Orange! *Orange who?*
Orange you glad I didn't say red?

Knock Knock. *Who's there?*
Turnip! *Turnip who?*
Turn up the heater, it's cold in here!

Knock Knock. *Who's there?*
Sarah! *Sarah who?*
Sarah 'nother way in?

Knock Knock. *Who's there?*
Tennis! *Tennis who?*
Tennis five plus five!

Knock Knock. *Who's there?*
Thumb! *Thumb who?*
Thumb people would just let me in!

Knock Knock. *Who's there?*
Vitamin! *Vitamin who?*
Vitamin for a party!

Knock Knock. *Who's there?*
Amos. *Amos who?*
Amos-quito.

Knock Knock. *Who's there?*
Jacqueline. *Jacqueline who?*
Jacqueline Hyde.

Knock Knock. *Who's there?*
Alpaca. *Alpaca who?*
Alpaca lunch for the picnic.

MORE ANIMAL ANTICS

Which bird is always out of breath?
A puffin.

Why does a hummingbird hum?
It doesn't know the words!

What's black and white and very noisy?
A magpie with a drum kit.

What did the parrot say when it fell in love with the frog?
Polly wants a croaker!

What do owls sing when it's raining?
Too wet to woo.

What do vultures always have for dinner?
Leftovers.

How do hens dance?
Chick to chick.

How do you hire a horse?
Put four bricks under his feet.

Why do buffaloes always travel in herds?
Because they're afraid of getting mugged by elephants.

What does an echidna have for lunch?
Prickled onions.

Which type of bird steals from banks?
A robin.

ONE OF THOSE DANGEROUS BLACK SPACES BETWEEN THE WHITE ONES

Now you see it, now you don't, now you see it, now you don't. What is it?
A black cat on a zebra crossing.

Where do cats go to see exhibitions?
The mewseum.

What do you call a cat who loses a fight?
Claude.

What do you call fourteen rabbits hopping backwards?
A receding hareline.

What did the cat say when it lost all its money?
I'm paw.

What goes '99 bonk'?
A centipede with a wooden leg.

Why did the insects drop the centipede from their football team?
He took too long to put on his boots!

Why was the chicken sick?
Because it had people pox.

What do you call a crazy chicken?
A cuckoo cluck.

Why did the fool put a chicken in a hot bath?
So she would lay hard-boiled eggs.

I hate having to lay the hard boiled ones

What does a crab use to call someone?
A shellular phone!

What do you call a baby whale?
A little squirt.

What lives at the bottom of the sea with a six gun?
Billy the Squid.

What do you call a frog with no legs?
Unhoppy.

What is Kermit the Frog's middle name?
The.

Where do sick ponies go?
To the horsepital.

Why do frogs like beer?
Because it is made from hops.

What's the tallest yellow flower in the world?
A giraffodil.

Have you ever seen a man-eating tiger?
No, but in a restaurant I once saw a man eating chicken.

I play Scrabble with my pet dog every night.

He must be clever.

I don't know about that. I usually beat him.

What do you call a fly with no wings?
A walk.

What has four wheels and flies?
A garbage bin on wheels.

What do you call a mosquito that prefers walking to flying?
An itch-hiker.

How do fireflies start a race?
Ready, steady, glow!

How many ants are needed to fill an apartment?
Ten-ants.

Why did the termite quit its job?
Because it was boring.

Which insects can tell the time?
Clockroaches.

What has four legs and sees just as well from both ends?
A horse with his eyes closed.

What did the fish say when he swam into the wall?
Dam.

Does your dog bite?
No.
Oww. I thought you said your dog doesn't bite.
That's not my dog.

What song do lions sing at Christmas?
'Jungle bells'.

How do you stop a dog doing his business in the hall?
Put him outside.

Who went into the tiger's lair and came out alive?
The tiger.

What's the difference between a dark sky and an injured lion?
One pours with rain, the other roars with pain.

What happened to the leopard who took four baths every day?
Within a week he was spotless.

What does a caterpillar do on New Year's Day?
Turns over a new leaf.

What is a narrow squeak?
A thin mouse!

What did the duck say when she finished shopping?
Just put it on my bill.

Master Hog demonstrating his famous... Pork Chop.

AAAARR-YA

What do you call a pig that does karate?
Pork chop.

Who is emperor of all mice?
Julius Cheeser.

Why did the boy get in trouble for feeding the monkeys at the zoo?
Because he fed them to the lions.

What's black and white and goes round and round?
A penguin caught in a revolving door.

What do you give a pig with a rash?
Oinkment!

Which animals are best at maths?
Rabbits, because they're always multiplying.

What do you call a pig who enjoys jumping from a great height?
A stydiver.

Why did the parrot wear a raincoat?
Because it wanted to be polly unsaturated.

Why did the owl 'owl?
Because the woodpecker would peck 'er.

What do you call a cat that lives in a hospital?
A first aid kit.

MEOWW

FIRST AID KIT

What do you call a zebra without stripes?
A horse.

What is a sheep's favourite dessert?
A chocolate baaaaa.

Where do sheep shop?
At Woolworths.

What do you call a hippo that believes in peace, love and understanding?
A hippie-potamus.

What was the tortoise doing on the freeway?
About three metres an hour.

What did the judge say when he saw the skunk in the courtroom?
Odour in the court!

What is the difference between a wolf and a flea?
One howls on the prairie, the other prowls on the hairy.

What do snails apply before going on a date?
Snail varnish.

How do you make a snake cry?
Take away its rattle!

What do you do with a mouse that squeaks?
You oil him.

What's green and wiggly and goes 'hith'?
A snake with a lisp.

What sort of music is played most in the jungle?
Snake, rattle and roll.

What do you give to a sick snake?
An asp-rin.

What is a snake's favourite opera?
Wrigoletto.

Why did the viper vipe her nose?
Because the adder ad 'er 'ankerchief.

What's striped and goes round and round?
A zebra on a merry-go-round.

What do you get when you cross a high chair and a bird?
A stool pigeon.

What do get if you cross a centipede with a parrot?
A walkie-talkie.

What do you call a crate of ducks?
A box of quackers.

Definitely NOT a crate of ducks!

What do you call a pig with no clothes on?
Streaky bacon.

What do you get when you cross a chicken with a yo-yo?
A bird that lays the same egg three times!

What do get when you cross a dog and a cat?
An animal that chases itself.

What do you get when you cross a giraffe with an echidna?
A ten-metre toothbrush.

What do you get when you cross an eel with a shopper?
A slippery customer.

What do you get when you cross a frog with a small dog?
A croaker spaniel.

What do you get when you cross a dog with a vegetable?
A Jack brussel.

What do you get when you cross a monkey with a flower?
A chimp-pansy.

What do you get when you cross a black bird with a madman?
A raven lunatic.

What do you get when you cross a flea with a comedian?
A nitwit.

What do you get when you cross a kookaburra with a jug of gravy?
A laughing stock.

What is a parrot's favourite game?
Hide and speak.

AWESOME INSULTS

Janet: *'What's the difference between a cake and a school bus?'*

Jill: *'I don't know.'*

Janet: *'I'm glad I didn't send you to pick up my birthday cake!'*

You are so dumb, you saw a sign outside a police station that read 'Man Wanted for Robbery', and you went in and applied for the job!

You are so dumb you invented a chocolate teapot.

You are so dumb you fed money to your cow because you wanted to get rich milk.

You are so dumb you invented rubber nails.

You are so dumb you climbed over a glass wall to see what was on the other side.

Boy: *'They say ignorance is bliss.'*

Girl: *'Then you should be the happiest boy in the world!'*

You are so dumb, when you went hitchhiking you got up early so there wouldn't be much traffic around.

You are so dumb you tripped over a cordless phone.

You are so dumb, when you dress up as a pirate you put a patch over both eyes.

You are so dumb you have a stop sign at the top of your ladder.

You are so dumb you took a gun with you when you went white-water rafting, so you could shoot the rapids.

Your dad is so dumb he only gets a half-hour lunchbreak because if he took any longer he would have to be retrained.

You are not as stupid as you look. That would be impossible.

You have an open mind. Ideas just slip straight out.

Your brother is so dumb, when he swam across the English Channel he got tired halfway and swam back.

Your dad is so dumb he locked himself in a motorbike.

You are so dumb you fell out of a tree after you were told to rake up the leaves.

You are so dumb you threw the butter out of window because you wanted to see a butterfly.

You are as smart as bait.

How dare you tell everyone I'm stupid. *Sorry, I didn't realise it was a secret.*

I hear you were the last one born in your family. I can understand that. You're enough to discourage anyone.

You are so dumb, when you heard 90% of all accidents occur around the home you moved.

I know you are nobody's fool but maybe someone will adopt you.

I would ask you how old you are but I know you can't count that high.

If I ever need a brain transplant, I'd choose yours because I'd want a brain that had never been used.

Just because you have a sharp tongue that does not mean you have a keen mind.

You have a photographic mind. It's a pity it has never been developed.

You are so ugly they push your face into dough to make cookies.

You are so ugly they didn't give you a costume when you auditioned for *Star Wars*.

You are so ugly your mum had to tie a steak around your neck to get the dog to play with you.

Every time you open your mouth your foot falls out.

You are so dumb if you had a brain you'd take it out and play with it.

Woman: *'When I'm old and ugly, will you still love me?'*
Man: *'I do, don't I?'*

You are so ugly, when you went on a package tour near where headhunters live you were the only survivor.

Your sister is so ugly the garbage man won't even pick her up.

I'm not saying my wife isn't good looking but when she goes to the doctor he tells her to open her mouth and go 'Moooo'.

You are so dumb you think birds that are kept in captivity are called jail birds.

STATE CORRECTIONS
Killer Kanary
Z04302-B

If I were as ugly as you I'd wear a mask.

Your mum is so fat she's got smaller fat women orbiting around her.

Your mum is so fat they tie a rope around her shoulders and drag her through a tunnel when they want to clean it.

Your mum is so fat, when she goes to an all-you-can-eat buffet they have to install speed bumps.

Your mum is so fat she shows up on radar.

Your mum is so fat, when she leaves the beach everybody shouts, 'The coast is clear.'

Your mum is so fat, when she walked in front of the TV I missed three commercials.

Your mum is so fat she climbed Mt Everest with one step.

Your mum is so fat, when the police showed her a picture of her feet she couldn't identify them.

Your mum is so fat, when she tiptoes everyone yells, 'Stampede!'

You remind me of a camel.
Why?
You give me the hump.

First Man: *'My girlfriend eats like a bird.'*
Second Man: *'You mean she hardly eats a thing?'*
First Man: *'No, she eats slugs and worms.'*

When Wally Witherspoon proposed to his girlfriend, she said, *'I love the simple things in life, Wally, but I don't want one of them for a husband!'*

Your mum is so fat, when she went to get a waterbed they put a blanket across the Pacific Ocean.

A man walks into a bar with a skunk under his arm.
Barman: *'You can't bring that smelly thing in here.'*
Skunk: *'Sorry. I'll leave him outside.'*

You are so ugly, when you were born your mother said, 'What a treasure!' and your father said, 'Yes, let's go bury it.'

You are so dumb you think a fjord is a Scandinavian motor car.

You are so tight with your money you sit at the back of the bus to get a longer ride for your money.

Waiter, do you serve crabs in this restaurant?
Yes sir, we serve anyone.

'The girl who sits beside me in maths is very clever,' said Alec to his mother. 'She's got enough brains for two.' 'Perhaps you'd better think of marriage,' said his mum.

Your family is so poor, when I went inside your house I accidentally stepped on a cockroach and your whole family came out singing, 'Clap your hands, stomp your feet, thank the Lord that we got meat!'

Hey teacher, I'd be a foul person too if I had to look at us all day.

Your granddad is so old he can whistle and clean his teeth at the same time.

Do you like my cottage pie?
Umm, next time try taking the drains out first.

He has an answer for everything.
Yes, the wrong one.

Is it true your brother is an only child?

People like that don't grow on trees you know.
No, they normally swing under them.

Instead of drinking from the fountain of knowledge, you just gargled.

Jack: 'Mum, all the boys at school call me Big Head.'

Mum: 'Never mind, dear, just run down to the grocery store and collect the big bag of apples I ordered in your cap.'

You are like an oil well. Always boring.

Do you know what nice people do at the weekend?
No.
I didn't think you would.

I don't like soup.
I expect you can't get it to stay on the fork can you?

I love looking in the mirror admiring my looks. Do you think that's vanity?
No, just a vivid imagination.

Any similarity between you and a human is purely coincidental!

Hi, I'm a human being! What are you?

I bet your mother has a loud bark!

My doctor says I should give up football.
So he's seen you play too then.

You're so skinny, you could hang-glide on a corn chip.

Hi, I'm from Earth. Have we met?

How do you keep a nerd in suspense for 24 hours?
I'll tell you tomorrow.

When you were born the doctor slapped your mother.

His death won't be listed under 'Obituaries', more like 'Neighbourhood Improvements'.

First Girl: *'Whenever I'm down in the dumps, I buy myself a new hat.'*
Second Girl: *'Oh, so that's where you get them!'*

Your dad is so hairy, Big Foot takes pictures of him.

You will never be the man your mother is.

My dad is so mean with money he heats the knives so we don't use too much butter.

I do lots of exercise.
I thought so. That's why you're so long-winded.

How many people work in your office?
About half of them.

You are so dumb you burnt your ear because you were ironing when the phone rang.

You are so dumb you burnt your other ear when the caller rang back.

Mrs Johnston, your daughter would be a fine dancer, except for two things.
What are they?
Both feet!

I hear she is a business woman.
Yes, her nose is always in other people's business.

You are so dumb you went round and round in a revolving door looking for the doorknob.

You are so dumb you invented waterproof teabags.

You have the face of a saint. A Saint Bernard, that is.

You are so dumb you invented a mirror for ghosts.

You are so dumb you invented non-stick glue.

If a Scortsman was to weer underweer under his kilt...and I'm nort saying aye dooo... They'd be just like these prickly woollen tartan underpants

You are so dumb you invented underwear for kilt wearers.

You'll just have to give me credit. *Well I certainly won't be giving you cash.*

You are so dumb, when I asked you what the weather was like, you replied, 'It's too foggy to tell.'

You are so dumb, when you went shoplifting you stole a free sample.

You are so dumb, if you ever have a brain transplant, the brain will be sure to reject you.

You are so dumb, at Halloween you carve a face on an apple and go bobbing for pumpkins.

You are so dumb you left your job as a telephonist because you kept hearing voices.

Our goalkeeper is so dumb he won't catch the ball because he thinks that's what the net is for.

You are so dumb you think that a kilo of feathers weighs less than a kilo of lead.

Don't let your mind wander – it's too little to be let out alone.

Your mum is so dumb she put lipstick on her forehead because she wanted to make up her mind.

You are so dumb you ordered a cheeseburger without cheese.

You are a few fries short of a Happy Meal.

You forgot to pay your brain bill.

You are so dumb you put a coin in a parking meter and waited for a gumball to come out.

You are so dumb you ordered your sushi well done.

Go ahead, tell us everything you know. It'll only take 10 seconds.

You are so dumb you leapt from a window to try out your new jump suit.

Of course you need to read in the dark Robert... this is night school!

For a start... I'm not Robert. Robert's over there. Do you have a torch I can borrow to find my book Miss?

You are so dumb you went to night school to learn to read in the dark.

Are you always this stupid or are you making a special effort today?

You are so dumb you threw a rock at the ground, and missed.

You are so dumb you couldn't pour water out of a boot if the instructions were written on the bottom of the heel.

You obviously fell out of the Stupid Tree and hit every branch on the way down.

You are so dumb you push when playing tug of war.

Bill: *'My sister has lovely long hair, all down her back.'*
Will: *'Pity it's not on her head!'*

You are so ugly, when you enter a room the mice jump on chairs.

Haven't I seen you on TV?
Well yes, I do appear off and on. How do you like me?
Off.

You are so dumb you tiptoe past the medicine cabinet so that you don't wake the sleeping pills.

Can you cut out the snoring... I'm trying to get some sleep!

SLEEPING PILLS

After cruel taunts about having a head like a pumpkin... Peter opted for a quiet night in on Halloween.

Don't look out of the window. People will think that it's Halloween.

I've just come back from the beauty salon.
What a pity it was closed.

You are so ugly, when you walk into a bank they turn off the surveillance cameras.

You remind me of a calendar. Your days are numbered.

Your sister has everything a man desires – bulging muscles and moustache.

You smell funny.
That's my soap. I don't suppose you've smelt it before.

Your breath is so bad that people look forward to your farts.

Whisper those three little words that would make my day.
Get a life!

He's good at everything he does. And as far as I can see he usually does nothing.

You are so ugly even Rice Bubbles won't talk to you!

Do you think, Professor, that my girlfriend should take up the piano as a career?
No, I think she should put down the lid as a favour!

My dad is so mean with money he told us that when the ice-cream van plays music it has run out of ice-cream.

You are so careless, when you tried to fit a new window you broke it with a hammer.

As an outsider, what do you think of the human race?

You are so forgetful you wrote a letter to yourself and forgot to sign it. When it arrived, you didn't know who sent it.

I'll never forget the first time we met – although I keep trying.

You are so poor, when I went to your house and asked where the bathroom was you said, 'Third bottle to the left.'

You are lower than the fluff in an earthworm's belly button.

My girlfriend talks so much that when she goes on holidays she has to spread suntan lotion on her tongue!

Can you cure my fleas?
Maybe, what's wrong with them?

They call him 'Caterpillar' because he has got where he is by crawling.

I hear the team's prospects are looking up.
I didn't know you were leaving.

You are so dumb you thought Sherlock Holmes was a housing project.

Whenever I go to the store, they shake my hand.
I expect it's to make sure you don't put it in the till.

How long can someone live without a brain?
How old are you?

You're multi-talented. You do a hundred things badly.

I can play piano by ear.
And I can fiddle with my toes.

Your antenna isn't picking up all the channels.

You dad is so hairy they filmed *Gorillas in the Mist* in his shower.

How did you get here? Did someone leave your cage open?

I thought of you all day today. I was at the zoo.

When they made you they broke the mould. Then, they found the mould maker, dragged him out into the street and beat him up.

Your house is so nasty I tripped over a rat and a cockroach stole my wallet.

He loves his wife so much, not only did he put in a swimming pool, he even bought a shark to go in it.

You are so slow you have to speed up to stop!

When I look into your eyes, I can see cows grazing.

Are you just visiting this planet?

When you and your mum had an argument, it was a battle of the Wits – Nit versus Dim. When your dad joined in, it was Nit versus Dim verses Half.

When you were born your mother did not know which end to put the nappy on.

You are so dumb you think a polygon is a dead parrot.

You are so dumb you think Hamlet is an omelette with bacon.

You are so dumb you invented a glass baseball bat.

You are so dumb you invented an ejector seat on a helicopter.

You are so dumb you got your money back after having your mind read.

You are so dumb, when the lifesaver told you not to jump in the pool because there was no water, you replied, 'It's alright, I can't swim.'

You are so dumb, when I told you that your shoes had to be soled, you sold them.

You are so dumb you slept under your car because you wanted to wake up oily in the morning.

You are so dumb, when you went water-skiing you spent your whole holiday looking for a sloping lake.

You are so dumb you threw away your donut because it had a hole in the middle.

You are so dumb you forgot your twin brother's birthday.

You should go to a dentist and have some wisdom teeth put in.

Your dad is so dumb he took a ruler to bed to see how long he slept.

Your mum is so dumb, when you asked her to buy you a colour TV she asked, 'What colour?'

Your mum is so dumb, when she fills in forms that say 'Sign Here', she writes 'Taurus'.

You are an experiment in artificial stupidity.

Your sewing machine is out of thread.

I've changed my mind.
Great, does the new one work any better?

The cat that made off with the mouse...and the computer

You are so dumb you put your pet cat next to the computer to keep an eye on the mouse.

So a thought crossed your mind? Must have been a long and lonely journey.

You are the kind of friend a person can depend on. You're always around when you need me.

You're so dumb you can't even spell the word 'dumb'.

It's perfectly all right to have an unexpressed thought. In fact, in your case I recommend it.

People say you're a perfect idiot. I tell them you may not be perfect but you are doing a great job being an idiot.

Every time I take my girlfriend out for a meal, she eats her head off.
She looks better that way.

Last time I saw someone as ugly as you I had to pay admission.

Do you think that I'll lose my looks when I get older?
With luck, yes.

You're so unpopular even your answering machine hangs up on you.

Hello...This is your own answering machine. Don't bother to leave a message...just go away!

Someone told me you are not fit to live with pigs but I stuck up for you and said you were.

You are so ugly, when you stand on the beach the tide won't come in.

Either you're very ugly or your neck has stepped in something.

Is that a new perfume I smell?
It is, and you do.

You don't need to use an insult, you could just use your breath.

You are so lazy you got a job in a bakery to loaf around.

You're so lazy, that if you woke up with nothing to do, you'd go to bed with it only half done.

He is the kind of a man that you would use as a blueprint to build an idiot.

You don't know the meaning of the word 'fear', but then again you don't know the meaning of most words.

You are so ugly you made an onion cry.

My big brother is such an idiot. The other day I saw him hitting himself over the head with a hammer. He was trying to make his head swell, so his hat wouldn't fall over his eyes!

Person 1: *'I've never been so insulted in all my life.'*
Person 2: *'You haven't been trying.'*

You are such a bad typist you type sixty mistakes a minute.

You are such a bad cook even the maggots get takeaway.

You are growing on me – like a wart.

I am going to get a fur for you.
As fur as possible.

Your mum is so ugly your dad takes her to work with him so that he doesn't have to kiss her goodbye.

My sister has such a sharp tongue we don't need a knife to carve the Sunday roast.

What position do you play in the football team?
I'm not sure, though the coach calls me one of the drawbacks.

You remind me of a toenail. The sooner you get cut down to size the better.

Did your parents ever ask you to run away from home?

Mary: *'Do you think my sister's pretty?'*
Gary: *'Well, let's just say if you pulled her pigtail, she'd probably say, "Oink, oink!"'*

I've been asked to get married hundreds of times.
Yes, but your parents don't count.

Don't you have a terribly empty feeling – in your skull?

You are so scared you wear a lifejacket when you sleep on a waterbed.

I hear you were born on a farm. Any more in the litter?

I'm busy now. Can I ignore you some other time?

Is that your face or did your neck throw up?

You are as sharp as a bowling ball.

May a thousand fleas from a camel's back infest your armpit and keep you warm at night.

If I had a brother like you, I'd put myself up for adoption.

You're a legend in your own mind!

When I want your opinion I'll rattle your cage.

You remind me of the southernmost portion of a northern bound horse.

That isn't your forehead, it's your hair trying to run away from your face.

You are so short and hairy, when you walk around the house your mother screams, 'Mouse!'

You're not acting like yourself lately. I noticed the improvement immediately.

I've heard you're the big noise around here. I think you should cut back on the baked beans.

You are so dumb you got fired from your job as an elevator operator because you couldn't remember the route.

You might not know much but you lead the league in nostril hair.

You are so dumb you invented a parachute that opens on impact.

You are so dumb you ate a worm when you were asked to do a bird impression.

You are so dumb you called your pet zebra 'Spot'.

Boy: *'I'll tell you everything I know.'*
Girl: *'In that case you'll be speechless!'*

You are so dumb, when you went shoplifting you hurt your back trying to lift the corner store.

Your dad is so dumb, when he locked his keys in the car he called a mechanic to get the family out.

How many toes does an idiot have?
Take off your socks and count them.

You are so dumb it takes you three hours to watch 'Sixty Minutes'.

You are so dumb you kept banging your head against the wall because it felt so good when you stopped.

You are so dumb you asked for a price check at the $2 shop.

You are so dumb you tried to drown a fish.

You are a few clowns short of a circus.

You are so dumb, when you missed the 44 bus you took the 22 twice instead.

You are so dumb you invented a solar-powered flashlight.

He is living proof that man can live without a brain!

I bet your brain feels as good as new, seeing that you've never used it.

Your mum is so fat, when she sits on the beach Greenpeace shows up and tries to tow her back into the ocean.

You look lost in your thoughts – unfamiliar territory for you.

If you were any dumber you'd have to be watered twice a week.